Pirates of the West Indies

CLINTON V. BLACK, F.S.A.

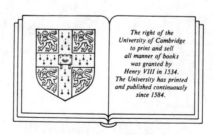

The right of the
University of Cambridge
to print and sell
all manner of books
was granted by
Henry VIII in 1534.
The University has printed
and published continuously
since 1584.

CAMBRIDGE UNIVERSITY PRESS

Cambridge

New York   Port Chester   Melbourne   Sydney

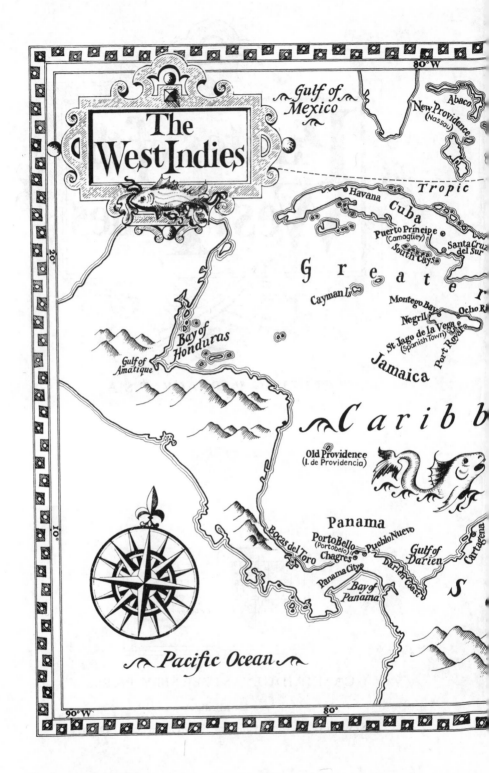

The West Indies

80°W

Gulf of Mexico

New Providence (Nassau)

Abaco

Tropic

Havana

Cuba

Puerto Príncipe (Camagüey)

Santa Cruz del Sur

South Cays

G r e a t e r

Cayman I.

Montego Bay

Ocho R.

Negril

St Jago de la Vega (Spanish Town)

Port Royal

Bay of Honduras

Jamaica

Gulf of Amatique

C a r i b b

Old Providence (I. de Providencia)

Panama

Bocas del Toro

PortoBello (Portobelo)

Pueblo Nuevo

Gulf of Darien

Cartagena

Chagres

Darien Coast

Panama City

Bay of Panama

S

Pacific Ocean

90°W

80°

For Anna

Published by the Press Syndicate of the University of Cambridge
The Pitt Building, Trumpington Street, Cambridge, CB2 1RP
40 West 20th Street, New York, NY 10011, USA
10 Stamford Road, Oakleigh, Melbourne 3166, Australia

First published 1989   Third printing 1990

Printed in Great Britain by Bell and Bain

British Library cataloguing in publication data
Black, Clinton V. (Clinton Vane)
Pirates of the West Indies.
1. Caribbean region. Pirates, history
I. Title
910.4′53
ISBN 0 521 35271 1 hard covers
ISBN 0 521 35818 3 paperback

Library of Congress cataloging-in-publication data
Black, Clinton Vane de Brosse, 1918–
Pirates of the West Indies/Clinton V. Black.
144 p. 23 cm.
Bibliography: 2 p.
Includes index.
ISBN 0 521 35818 3
1. Pirates – West Indies.   I. Title
G535.B55   1989
364.1′64–dc19
88-27449

V N

Acknowledgements

The verse from John Masefield's 'Cargoes' on page 2 is reproduced by permission of The Society of Authors as the literary representative of the Estate of John Masefield and by permission of Macmillan Publishing Company, New York.
The Publishers also wish to thank the following for their permission to reproduce illustrations:
The owner of the original painting of Henry Morgan, 'The Buccaneer', which is reproduced on the back cover; Newport Borough Council, for the portrait of Henry as a young man, reproduced on page 28 (the original painting now hangs in Tredegar House, Newport). Special thanks are due to Emlyn Magness, for bringing the existence of these paintings to our notice, and for his help in acquiring copies of them.
The National Maritime Museum for the illustrations on pages 4, 20, 26, 30, 52, 61, 89, 105, 108.
The Jamaica Archives for the illustration on page 115.

Maps, titles and illustration on page 22 by Celia Hart.
Illustration on page 129 by Clyde Pearson.
Cover illustration by Chris Ryley.

Contents

Foreword

Piracy reached its peak in the West Indies in the decade 1714 to 1724, with operations stretching up the eastern seaboard of the American colonies, north as far as Newfoundland and south and east to the slave coast of West Africa. In this short span of time as many perhaps as 5,500 men were engaged in the business. To select a dozen or so practitioners to represent the period is no easy task. All the same, of this large company who sailed under the Banner of King Death, as they called their dreaded ensign, the majority were destined to play supporting roles to the relatively few principal actors.

Here the forerunners are represented by the buccaneers Henry Morgan, the most outstanding, and Richard Sawkins, of the Pacific Venture fame. Here is the greatest pirate of all, Bartholomew Roberts, who captured 400 ships and brought the trade of the Americas to a standstill; Howel Davis, the most daring and ingenious of the Welsh pirate wizards; George Lowther whose operations ranged over the whole area, only to end in the solitude of a lignum vitae grove on a deserted Caribbean island; Charles Vane who, deposed from one command, went on to carve out a second successful career and, when that ended, strode to the gallows 'without the least remorse'; Edward Teach, the most notorious pirate of his day, whose great black beard 'frightened America more than any comet'; the dashing 'Calico' Jack Rackham whose fame owed not a little to his female crew members; John Evans, typical of the small entrepreneurs, who started his career with a canoe and three cronies; and, finally, Nicholas Brown, the 'Grand Pirate', whose story, contained largely in the Jamaica Archives, is now told here in full. William Kidd, perhaps the best known pirate of all, and the remarkable Henry 'Long Ben' Every (or Avery) must receive passing mention only as their main theatre of operations lay largely outside the geographical scope of this book.

A difficulty which faces the pirate author is, as Philip Gosse says, 'the diffidence shown by his heroes in recording their own deeds'. Apart then from such information as is to be found in official archival sources, a heavy reliance must be placed on the two classic works on the subject, *The Buccaneers of America* by Alexander Esquemeling (1678) and the *History of the Pirates* by Captain Charles Johnson, *alias* Daniel Defoe (1724). Seventeenth-century spelling was very elastic and only a little less so in the eighteenth. In direct quotations from both authors I have retained the original spelling and in general modernized the use of capitals. When quoting Defoe I have used his pen name of Captain Charles Johnson, throughout.

I wish to thank the staffs of the University Library of the West Indies, Mona, and the National Library of Jamaica. I am much indebted to my old friend and former colleague Geoffrey Yates who read the manuscript and made a number of important suggestions; but I owe most of all to my wife Anna whose book this is.

C.V.B.

Under the Banner of King Death

Few subjects have cast a stronger spell over the imagination of mankind than the exploits and desperate daring of the pirates, especially those of the West Indies where piracy reached unequalled heights.

In the minds of many the popular picture of the pirate tends to be a highly romantic one. It is the picture of a flamboyant, swashbuckling seafarer, with big gold earrings, a black eyepatch, a bandana, magnificent boots, a large curved cutlass in one hand and a brace of pistols tucked into a broad belt; the picture of a daredevil, scarfaced seawolf, amassing a fortune in gold and jewels; of a rakehell ashore, drinking and whoring in some secluded cove or pirate port. Not unnaturally, however, their contemporaries failed to appreciate these romantic features.

To the victims of piracy – the passengers and crew of some luckless merchantman, attacked and looted by a fierce and ruthless bunch of men – the picture was different. Piracy was a serious crime, the judicial penalty for which was death. The pirate was, in the words of the ancient statute, *hostis humani generis*: 'a common enemy'. He stole from all (except from his own kind) and held authority from none; he sailed under no national flag and was outside the law of his own nation.

This is the other side of the picture which moved one writer on the subject to describe pirates as 'abominable brutes', and another, writing in 1837, as 'monsters in human form'. But this, too, is a distortion and suffers also from the common error of judging the past by the moral fashions of the present.

The noted authority on pirates and piracy, Philip Gosse, put the picture into better perspective when he wrote: 'Piracy at its greatest moments becomes a major part of history itself but even in its lesser phases there is a fascination that is peculiarly its own, apart even from the spell that crime can exercise on the imagination. For it is a crime of a very special sort, demanding of its followers much more than boldness, cunning or skill in the use of arms.'

Piracy is as old as mankind, as old as boats, and is inextricably intertwined with travel and trade. Mediterranean piracy throve in the days of Ancient Rome. The youthful Julius Caesar was kidnapped by pirates in 78 BC while on a voyage to Rhodes and held for ransom. The ransom paid, Caesar returned later, captured the corsair crew and ordered every one of them to be executed. At this period piracy was largely the business of kidnapping for purposes of ransom, with captured passengers and crew the principal prize. Those not ransomable were invited to lighten ship by making their own way ashore – the origin, perhaps, of the myth of 'walking the plank' which appears to have no basis in fact.

The Phoenicians were early on the pirate scene, while the Vikings (their very name stems from their marauding activities) swarmed south from their icy northern territories to ravage and plunder the coasts of Britain, Ireland and France from the eighth to the tenth centuries AD.

With the expulsion of the Moors from Spain in 1492, the north coast of Africa became the staging place for the Barbary pirates, with the main strongholds at Tripoli, Algiers and Sallee (now Salé). Starting as an anti-Spanish campaign, the activities of these dreaded pirates, especially in the sixteenth century under the leadership of the red-bearded Turkish Barbarossa brothers, became a sort of holy war against all Christian nations. From their strongholds they sailed out to harry passing ships, to plunder the coasts of Spain and to take Christian captives to sell or work as slaves. Their activities lead us into almost indescribable dimensions of misery and suffering. Despite a number of expeditions sent against them, the operations of the Barbary pirates were not checked until 1830.

For many years the Red Sea Arabs proved past masters in the art of piracy, as did the Chinese and Malays, while the Pirate Coast of the Persian Gulf was dreaded by all honest seamen.

Throughout the Tudor reigns piracy was rampant around the British Isles, while during the adventurous years of Queen Elizabeth I, many Englishmen of position and birth went cruising on the Spanish Main in the hope of capturing some

> Stately Spanish galleon coming from the Isthmus,
> Dipping through the Tropics by the palm-green shores,
> With a cargo of diamonds,
> Emeralds, amethysts,
> Topazes, and cinnamon, and gold moidores.
>
> from 'Cargoes' by John Masefield

It is said that out of these semi-pirate adventurers evolved the buccaneers, themselves forerunners of the West Indian pirates, but the line of descent is not always clear, while anomalies of practice often clouded the nice distinctions since in many cases the same men were at different times buccaneers, privateers and pirates.

That particular school of piracy, buccaneering, and its later manifestations, especially privateering, was the direct outcome of Spain's impractical policy of forbidding her colonists the right to trade with other nationals, in spite of her own inability to supply their needs – a policy which, as it happened, other European nations were themselves to duplicate, if perhaps less rigidly, when they gained colonies of their own. It was the necessity for such clandestine trade which accounted for the success of John Hawkins, of Francis Drake (his first exploit in 1573 netted £40,000 in silver, gold and pearls) and of others of their kind.

On the discovery of the New World by Christopher Columbus, Pope Alexander VI had issued a proclamation dividing the Indies between Spain and Portugal, but it was not long before the northern sea powers began challenging the justice of this arbitrary division. Columbus had opened the way west and in his wake came the seafaring adventurers of many nations.

As early as 1506 French ships appeared in the Caribbean, attacking small Spanish settlements and capturing Spanish vessels. By 1542 the Dutch were trading in these waters. The English came late into the region and it was not until the ingenious John Hawkins organized his four trading voyages between 1562 and 1568 that England began to make a serious effort to break Spain's trade monopoly of the New World.

Up to the end of the sixteenth century the only settled colonies in the Americas were those of Spain. So far the challenge by other European nations to Spanish claims in the area had taken the form of raiding and smuggling, but soon a more serious threat appeared when the intruders began to colonize the forbidden territory and establish firm trade links with their Spanish neighbours.

The first English experiments in colonization started at the beginning of the seventeenth century, in Virginia, Bermuda (by accident of shipwreck) and Guiana – the coastal area between the Spanish possessions on the Orinoco and those of Portugal on the Amazon. But it was not until 1624 that the first permanent English settlement in the West Indies was started, by Thomas Warner in St Kitts. This was followed by the settling of Barbados three years later, of Nevis in 1628 and of Antigua and Montserrat in 1632. Jamaica fell to a Cromwellian privateering expedition in 1655. This undeclared war, which often continued in the Caribbean after peace treaties had been signed in Europe, was commonly referred to by the seamen of the time as 'no peace beyond the line' – an imaginary line outside the territorial limits of European treaties.

Pag 84.

Buccaneers of Hispaniola

Meanwhile a fraternity of freelance traders, soon to be known as *buccaneers*, arose on the otherwise uninhabited north and west parts of Hispaniola (which is now shared by Haiti and the Dominican Republic). They were men of many nations but mainly French, English and Dutch, and of many types – runaway bondsmen driven to desperation by brutal treatment (it is estimated that between 1668 and 1671 alone, Jamaica lost 2,600 men to the buccaneers), castaways, escaped criminals, political and religious refugees, wanderers of every stripe and kind – who had set aside all national rivalries.

In the forests of Hispaniola roamed large herds of pigs and wild cattle, descendants of the domestic animals introduced by the early settlers, and at first the chief trade of the buccaneers was limited to the slaughtering of these beasts to provide cured meat, hides and tallow which they supplied to the ships that put in occasionally at the ports along the coast, in exchange for gunpowder, lead bullets, clothing, liquor and other rough stores. They hunted with the help of lean, savage dogs and for weapons used knives and long-barrelled muzzle-loaders, or 'buccaneering-pieces'. They were superb marksmen and prided themselves on being able to hit a coin spinning in mid-air. Later, when they took to the sea, they worked on the tactical rule that four muskets were as good as one big gun. They usually worked in pairs, each man having a mate (known as a *matelot*), with whom everything was shared. The name *buccaneer* comes from the French word *boucan* (adapted from a Carib term) referring to the frame used by these men for curing their meat, the method being to lay the meat, cut in long strips, on a hurdle of green wood to dry over a slow fire fed with the fat and bones of the slaughtered beasts.

Their life was rough and hard in the extreme, and although they have been called a community of fierce and filthy men, the fact is that they harmed no one. The Spanish, however, resented their presence in Hispaniola and tried to round them up with the help of lancers, without much success. An attempt to starve them into subjection by destroying or dispersing the animals they hunted had more effect, but the Spaniards were to pay dearly for their success. Driven from their peaceful occupation and filled with hatred of their Spanish persecutors, the buccaneers were to become butchers not of beasts but of men.

Around 1630 they moved to the small, rocky neighbouring island of Tortuga, 'Turtle Island', two miles off the north-west coast of Hispaniola and close to the northern entrance of the Windward Passage. The Spaniards soon rooted them out, but they were back the moment the coast was clear. Recognizing that their best hope of survival lay in unity, the buccaneers banded together into the *Confederacy of the Brethren of the Coast* and took to the sea. At first they used the only vessels to hand – light craft, mainly canoes – but captured Spanish ships taken by surprise attack soon swelled their small fleet, while with captured arms and guns they fortified Tortuga. Early successes brought them a flock of recruits, and the stronger and bolder they grew the farther they ranged.

Hundreds of books have been written about buccaneering and piracy, all, with few exceptions, squarely based on the two classics of pirate literature: *The Buccaneers of America* by Alexander Olivier Exquemelin (anglicized as Esquemeling) published in Amsterdam in 1678, the first English edition appearing six years later; and *A General History of the Robberies and Murders of the Most Notorious Pyrates* by Captain Charles Johnson (identified as Daniel Defoe), first published in London in 1724. Both have been shown to contain much accurate information and, together, they cover the most important periods of the age of piracy. Both authors wrote to entertain and a weakness in their work springs from the mistaken belief that to write about criminals one must be a moralist as well as a historian.

Defoe, author of *Robinson Crusoe* and *Moll Flanders*, was both novelist and historian, and it is up to the reader to decide where the novelist improves on the historian and (as with Esquemeling) where an obviously fictitious conversation is introduced to elaborate an historical fact.

Esquemeling was a Frenchman from Honfleur in Normandy. He went to Tortuga in 1666 as a young apprentice in the service of the French West India Company. This at best amounted to slavery, but he had the additional misfortune to fall into the hands of the governor of the island who treated him so brutally that his health broke down completely. Fearing that he would lose his investment should Esquemeling die, the governor sold him cheaply to a surgeon who proved as humane as the governor was cruel, and with whom Esquemeling regained his health, learning at the same time the mysteries of the barber-surgeon's art.

He enlisted on board a buccaneer ship in 1668 and, in addition to his surgical duties, must have made copious notes for his famous book on the Brethren of the Coast. Although he was in all the great buccaneering exploits he disliked the trade and hated the greatest buccaneer of them all – Henry Morgan.

It is to Esquemeling that we owe the account of the daring exploit of Pierre Le Grand, himself a Frenchman, native of Dieppe, which marks the real beginning of buccaneering. Pierre had been prowling in the Caribbean in a small boat with a crew of only twenty-eight, without taking a prize.

Now with provisions dangerously low, driven by hunger, thirst and greed for gain, they spotted one of the galleons of the Spanish Vice-Admiral's fleet near Cape Tiburón, on the west coast of Hispaniola, that had become separated from its fellows and which Pierre decided to attack. The buccaneers had developed the low-on approach to a ship's quarter where they were safe from her guns and could take a heavy toll of the deck hands with cannon and musket fire as they jammed the vessel's rudder and boarded. Pierre opted for stealth. Relentlessly he stalked the great galleon until the tropical night closed in, then, drawing near, he ordered the surgeon to bore holes in the bottom of their own small craft to ensure that there could be no turning back. Armed with sword and pistol Pierre and his men climbed silently on bare feet up the side of the galleon, dispatched the sleepy helmsman before he could blink, then dashing down to the great cabin burst in on the astonished captain playing cards with some of his officers. Pressing a pistol to the captain's chest Pierre ordered him to surrender the ship as the terrified Spaniards cried out: 'Jesus bless us! Are these devils or what are they?' – a cry that was to echo down the years.

Meanwhile others of the pirates had taken possession of the gun room, murdering every Spaniard who resisted them. As their own small craft filled with water and sank with a sucking sound beneath the blue Caribbean, Pierre Le Grand, standing barefoot on the deck of the great galleon, must have shouted with joy at the remarkable feat he and a mere handful of his countrymen had achieved.

He then did a thing seldom repeated in the history of the buccaneers. Resisting the strong temptation to return in triumph to Tortuga, to the pleasures of the taverns and stews, he set sail across the Atlantic for his home town of Dieppe where he retired on the rich proceeds of the galleon and her cargo. Pierre was an important pioneer. His success brought a steady flow of recruits to the ranks of the buccaneers.

Although lawless by calling, the buccaneers had a stern code of discipline which welded them into a formidable fighting force. They usually sailed under carefully drawn-up articles, the first of which was *No purchase* (a euphemism for loot), *no pay*. All plunder went into a common collection and was then divided according to share-out scales and disability pensions, as stated in the articles. This is important as forming the basis of the articles under which the pirates later sailed. The loss of a right arm in battle, for instance, brought a compensation of 600 pieces-of-eight or six slaves; the loss of a finger, one slave or 100 pieces-of-eight.

Much has been written about the cruelties of the buccaneers. It is reported of the Frenchman Francis L'Olonnais, for example, that he tortured prisoners to force them to tell where they had hidden their money and valuables and tore out their tongues if they resisted. On one occasion, after failing to get the desired information, he slit open the breast of a Spaniard with his cutlass and, tearing out the victim's heart, bit and gnawed it. His end shows a certain grim justice. He was captured by Darien Indians who tore him to pieces while he still lived, throwing his body bit by bit into the fire and his ashes into the air 'to the intent that no trace or memory might remain of such an infamous, inhuman creature'. He is, in fact, remembered for much else. He was the true forerunner of Henry Morgan, and his sacking of the cities of Maracaibo and Gibraltar on the Spanish Main was the first large-scale combined operation of the buccaneers.

The Dutchman Roche Brasiliano, another buccaneer captain, is said to have roasted several Spaniards alive upon wooden spits because they would not show him where they had their hogyards. Montbars of Languedoc in France, who was to go down in history as 'The Exterminator', at least claimed a moral sanction for his sadism: he joined the buccaneers with the sole intention of punishing the Spaniards for their cruelty to the American natives, about which he had read. Dedicating his life and sword to vengeance, he treated all Spaniards that fell into his hands with the utmost brutality. One of his favourite methods of torture was to cut his victim's belly open and extract one end of his guts which he nailed to a post. Burning wood pressed to the man's bare buttocks forced him into a ghastly dance of death to the limit of his insides, or his endurance.

It should be mentioned that Esquemeling, from whom many of these atrocity stories come, also relates horrifying accounts of the cruelty of planters towards their slaves and white indentured servants or bondsmen. Even if these chillingly cruel stories are true – and there is reason to believe they were exaggerated – before balancing the buccaneer's account, it can only be fairly judged against the life of the times and in relation to the behaviour of their law-enforcing contemporaries at home and their law-abiding contemporaries at sea. They lived in an age of appalling brutality. Many of them – L'Olonnais was one – laboured as bondsmen on West Indian plantations where they learnt lessons of cruelty by suffering it. Whatever else they might have been and whatever their crimes, the buccaneers were first-rate fighting men, reckless, fearless and desperate in their courage with a highly developed consciousness of kind, while their impressive rise to power during the seventeenth century was to prove a dominant factor in West Indian history.

Esquemeling has much to tell us of the wild deeds of the buccaneer ashore. Roche Brasiliano, for example, who was a renowned leader at sea, often went to pieces when on land: 'being in drink, he would run up and down the streets, beating or wounding whom he met, no person daring to oppose him or make any resistance . . . Such of these pirates', he continues, 'are found who will spend 2 or 3 thousand pieces-of-eight in one night, not leaving themselves peradventure a good shirt to wear on their backs in the morning. Thus upon a certain time I saw one of them give unto a common strumpet five hundred pieces-of-eight only that he might see her naked.'

In Port Royal, Jamaica, situated at the seaward end of the gaunt Palisadoes peninsula that shelters Kingston's fine harbour, the buccaneers soon found what they needed most: a ready market for their Spanish spoil, facilities for the repair and equipping of their ships and all the opportunities they desired for amusing themselves in brothel and tavern, and so flocked in ever growing numbers to the port.

They were alternately welcomed and discouraged by the Jamaica government, according to the dictates of Britain's changing foreign policy, but Jamaica stood to lose most when the buccaneers were out of favour for, driven from Port Royal, they simply carried their Spanish prizes and booty to Tortuga. Besides, in the absence of British naval units based on the island, it was comforting to have these searovers around since by their ceaseless, savage attacks on the neighbouring Spanish territories they kept the enemy occupied defending their own coasts, weakened Spain's control in the Caribbean and contributed in no small measure to the protection of the English as well as the French and Dutch colonies.

Sir Thomas Modyford, a wealthy Barbadian planter who became governor of Jamaica in 1664, began by suppressing the buccaneers, but the outbreak of the Second Dutch War the following year caused an about-turn in policy. The defence of the islands had to be based on the buccaneers and Modyford set to work organizing them into a striking force, furnishing each buccaneer captain with a commission known as a *Letter of Marque*, to make their activities legal and change their status to that of privateers.

The French had earlier tried using the buccaneers as organized irregulars, but without marked success; Modyford's early attempts were to prove no better. He gathered a force of ten ships and 500 men and dispatched it under General Edward Morgan (uncle of the famous Henry) to attack the Dutch islands of St Eustatius and Saba, whence, if successful, they should go on to Curaçao, but the project was too ambitious a one for so undisciplined a company. The buccaneers sailed on the usual 'no purchase, no pay' condition and so looked for personal profit before serving any other cause.

9

St Eustatius and Saba were captured easily enough, but disputes over the loot and the death of the elderly leader from heat and exertion caused the rest of the project to fall through.

It was in Henry Morgan that Modyford was to find the tough, resourceful young buccaneer-leader who could hold the wild Brethren together and direct their main efforts in the path that policy dictated.

The buccaneers may be said to have been the forerunners of the West Indian pirates, but once the original cow-killers took to the sea to hit back at their Spanish persecutors, titles become less clear-cut. Even before that another name had crept in: the French form was *filibustier*, anglicized as 'filibuster' or 'freebooter'. A basic distinction between buccaneer and pirate was that the former carried the war to the Spanish only, whereas the pirate attacked and stole from all and owed authority to none. When, however, the European governments made privateers of the buccaneers in time of war, open or undeclared (as they were later to do, from time to time, with the pirates) by arming them with commissions, their range widened, as in the case of Modyford's use of the buccaneers against the Dutch.

Henry Morgan always sailed with a commission, but to the Spaniards he was a pirate, nevertheless. His great predecessor, Sir Francis Drake, was commissioned by his monarch and was therefore a privateer. He became a national hero and his activities were viewed as grand and knightly adventures, but Philip II's Ambassador to the English Court, in a complaint to Queen Elizabeth, described him as 'the master-thief of the unknown world'. Later a certain Scotsman named John Paul Jones who was to become a renowned naval hero to the Americans in their War of Independence, was considered a pirate by the British.

Many commissions were not worth the paper they were written on. Some governors, such as that of Petit Goâve in Hispaniola, issued blank commissions for the recipient to fill in as he fancied! Other French commissions were merely permits to fish, fowl or hunt. Small wonder that some Spanish governors hung the commissions around the necks of buccaneers whom they succeeded in catching and executing.

> My commission is large and I
>   made it myself,
> And the capstan shall stretch it
>   full larger by half . . .

runs a ballad on the famous pirate Henry Every.

If the frequent shifts of political policy made it expedient for the governments to play fast and loose with the Brethren, they themselves had no illusions about their own motives: they were prepared to risk their lives, not in the defence of a country, but for gain. After the Treaty of Madrid in 1670, by which Britain's claim to Jamaica was recognized, the incidence of illegal attacks declined, while with the Treaty of Ryswyck twenty-seven years later, by which Hispaniola (or St Domingue, as it was now called) was formally ceded to France, the new governor Jean du Casse set about with characteristic firmness and efficiency replacing privateering with peaceful trade, cattle hunting and planting, compelling the remaining buccaneers in Tortuga to evacuate the island and settle in St Domingue. Himself an ex-buccaneer, du Casse had launched a formidable invasion of Jamaica in 1694 which was, however, beaten off. Like Henry Morgan, he was much honoured by his country and rewarded with high office.

With the Peace of Ryswyck the great age of the buccaneers might be said to have ended. But old habits die hard, and the stage was now being set for the era of piracy. As shown later in this book in the career of Captain Richard Sawkins, the old-guard freebooters were to find a convenient overland route through the Isthmus of Panama to the South Sea and to reap much profit from attacks on the Spanish Pacific coastal cities. Meanwhile 'wide-ranging English fleets' discovered the riches of the East carried in the European East Indiamen and by Mogul and Arab fleets. An impression of the extent and power of these pirates may be had from the exploits of Every, whose crowning achievement was the capture of the Great Mogul's flagship in the Indian Ocean which carried booty including 100,000 pieces-of-eight, 100,000 gold chequeens, a fortune in precious stones – and the Mogul's daughter! Then there are the privateering adventures of William Kidd, probably the best known pirate of all. These activities are enhanced by the strange myth of a pirate commonwealth in Madagascar, a communistic Utopia called *Libertalia*, established by a pirate named Mission who, we are told, founded his republic on the stirring principles of Liberty, Equality, Fraternity, sixty years before the French Revolution – a republic which probably existed only in Defoe's imagination, the whole invention, perhaps, being a carefully considered attack on the abuses of his time while expressing a pirate's dream world.

Piracy was to reach its peak in the West Indies and North America during the first half of the eighteenth century with more men (there were two notable women also) engaged in the business than anywhere else. It was estimated then that the pirate population varied from 1,000 to 2,000 at any given time; in all perhaps as many as 5,500 men sailed under the 'Banner of King Death', as they called their dreaded black flag. The reasons for this were many, the main being the rich prizes to be taken, the difficulty of pursuit of the small, swift pirate vessels by heavier men-of-war, and the abundance of cays, creeks and long stretches of undeveloped coastline affording facilities for lurking, surprise attack and escape, as well as for watering, provisioning, careening and carousing.

The Bahamas, with its nest of countless islands, cays and reefs, was the ideal base from which to pounce on merchantmen making their way through the Windward Passage or Florida Channel. So it was here, in the early 1690s, with their headquarters at New Providence (the Nassau of today), that the English pirates set up their commonwealth – successor to the buccaneer's Tortuga, and miniature Madagascar of the West. With its influx of traders, merchants and prostitutes, West Indian piracy was to flourish here until the 1720s when Britain finally established a settled government over the islands.

With an eye on trade and the weather, the pirates tended to move with the seasons, as far north as the docking areas of Newfoundland and down to the African Guinea Coast, at that time the centre of the thriving slave trade. So successful were they that by 1718 commerce in the West Indies and North America had been brought to a virtual standstill. In the three years between 1719 and 1722, Bartholomew Roberts, regarded as the most successful pirate of all, captured some 400 ships! It has been suggested that his death, doing battle with a naval frigate, and the capture of his crew, symbolized the end of piracy's golden age.

A number of factors played a part in fostering piracy. These included the Navigation Act, passed by Britain in 1696, the intent of which, in spite of the Spanish experience, was the exclusion of all nations, except England, from trading with English colonies. This added enormously to the cost of imports and encouraged the colonists, especially those of North America, to take to cheap, illegal buying wherever possible – the pirates, who were able to sell them products of the world's markets at the lowest prices, being their chief suppliers. As the 'trade' grew, pirate resorts sprang up in the Carolinas and the New England states, with the authorities, many of them corrupt, unable or unwilling through need or greed, to do anything about them. It was up to the British Navy to suppress piracy, but in peacetime the service was undermanned and inadequate for the job. This aside, the captains were far from conscientious, being too busy making money by trade. The Duke of Portland, governor of Jamaica from 1722 to 1726, writing to the Secretary of State about the naval officers of the time, complained that 'instead of clearing away the pirates [they] go from place to place with the sloops that are their own a tradeing, and when they have done come into harbour again, till they supply themselves with fresh goods.'

Portland's predecessor in office, the plain-spoken Sir Nicholas Lawes, reported sarcastically in 1719: 'I am sorry to have it to say, that His Majesty's ships of war attending this Island have either been so stationed as not to have been in the way of the pirates and Spaniards, or else had the misfortune not to meet with them.'

Who became pirates, and why? Père Labat, a Jesuit priest and respected authority on the subject, writing shortly after the end of the buccaneer era, tells us: 'The pirates are, as a rule, filibusters who have grown so accustomed to this free life in times of war, when they generally hold commissions, that they cannot make up their minds to return to work when peace is made, and therefore continue their roving.'

In that sense pirates were ordinary, normal seamen, but not all pirates started as privateers. The vast majority were recruited from the crews of captured merchantmen, some were mutineers and others were deserters or demobilized naval ratings. Many a celebrated pirate started on his own in a small way, as is illustrated by the account of Captain John Evans. Another remarkable example of these was Captain Richard Worley who set off on his short but prosperous career in 1718 in a small open boat with eight cronies, a few biscuits, a keg of water and a dozen old muskets. Some transported criminals and escaped bondsmen sought safety of a kind among the pirates, as they did in the days of the buccaneers, but others turned pirate for other reasons, the most unusual being Major Stede Bonnet, a wealthy Barbadian proprietor, who went 'on the account' to escape from a nagging wife!

In general seamen did not take to piracy for the love of it. They preferred privateering, but when a war ended and privateer crews were thrown out of work, many had little choice of employment. Piracy offered the prospects of quick gain, a free and easy life and escape from the harsh discipline of the naval and merchant services, especially the severe floggings which drove many seamen to desert and join pirate vessels.

The popular image of 'Jolly Jack Tar' had little relevance to the real existence of seamen in the first half of the eighteenth century. Their lives were governed by man-made and natural dangers. On land there was the ever present menace of the crimp and the press gang; at sea, apart from the normal hazards of seafaring, disease and accidents were commonplace in Jack's occupation. He squirmed under the iron hand of the captain, both naval and mercantile, ate abominable food while it lasted and anything that came to hand when that ran out on a long voyage, was worked often only for the sake of working and was paid a pittance at the end, assuming the captain paid up at all or that Jack lived long enough to collect.

The brutality of captains was unbelievably vicious. Discipline was so severe on the ships of the East India Company that the quarterdeck where floggings were carried out was described as resembling a 'slaughter house'. The records of the High Court of Admiralty are eloquent on the subject of the appalling beatings sailors received at the hands of their captains. One Richard Desbrough claimed that his captain beat him with his fist, ropes, sticks and canes and 'cut out one of his eyes'. Among the many cases of the kind that came before the Jamaica Court of Vice-Admiralty was that of William Floyd, master of the slaver *Indian Queen*, indicted for the murder of five of his crew. One was beaten to death by Floyd with his hands, fists and feet, one was forced overboard and drowned, the third was flogged to death, the fourth flogged and drowned, and the fifth killed by 'an instrument of iron called the tormentors'. None of the charges was made to stick.

In their articles and general organization the pirates ensured their freedom from such tyranny and despotism, especially in the control of their chosen captain. In Charles Johnson's words, 'They only permit him to be captain on condition that they may be captain over him.' He was selected for his courage, seamanship, fighting knowledge and luck. To be 'pistol-proof', as they put it, was a marked advantage. But the pirates went further. Reacting to the often violent and arbitrary authority of merchant captains, when a prize was taken they enquired closely into the treatment the crew had received from their captain, and those against whom complaint was made were punished by being whipped on their bare backs or shot through the head, depending on the charges laid against them. This was known as the 'Distribution of Justice'.

It was this same embittered response to the treatment meted out to seamen on naval and merchant vessels that engendered in the pirates a spirit of revenge. This is reflected in the very names they chose for their ships, and the frequency with which they went out of their way to avenge an insult or injury.

Opinions differ as to the level of discipline among the pirates. The fact is, as Marcus Rediker points out, with the pirates, discipline was less arbitrary than that of the merchant service and less codified than that of the navy; it 'depended on a collective sense of transgression'. Although, as their articles show, some crimes were punished by death, many misdeeds were accorded 'what Punishment the Captain and Majority of the Company shall think fit'. The highest authority on a pirate ship was the council to which were generally reserved decisions affecting the welfare of the crew and such matters as where the best prizes might be taken and the settling of dissensions. Some crews used the council a great deal; with others it was set up more as a court. However employed, its decisions were inviolable and seldom challenged by even the boldest of captains.

Whereas privateers were underwritten by promoters who expected fifty percent (or at least a third) of all plunder taken, a pirate ship was owned by the crew, to whom all spoil belonged according to a share-out scale, with a captain elected by the whole company. The ship was run along democratic lines which were almost anarchical, with a comradely distribution of life chances. The pirate's trade was a risky one, but all seafaring at that time had its hazards. Piracy was crime on a massive scale, the penalty for which was death by hanging – 'seen off at Wapping Old Stairs' (Execution Dock, in London), as the expression was. Patrick Pringle estimates, however, that in the peak pirate periods the number of men caught was probably less than one in a thousand, Charles Johnson notwithstanding, who informs us that 'the far greater part of these rovers are cut short in the pursuit, by a sudden precipitation into the other world'. But Johnson was writing mainly of the few who stood trial, while the great majority were anonymous and died in battle, by drowning or from natural causes.

Before setting off on a piratical voyage – 'going on the account' as it was called – all hands had to subscribe to a set of articles, with the usual basic condition being *no prey, no pay*. All loot went into a common pool. The captain was entitled to two full shares; the quartermaster, who was next in rank but was in fact the most important officer in the crew whose interests he was elected to represent and protect, received one-and-a-half shares, as did the master (or sailing master) who ranked third in importance; while the surgeon (if there was one), gunner and boatswain received one-and-a-quarter shares each. Included in the articles also was the typical disability clause providing compensation for injury received in action.

Among the unforgivable crimes in a pirate company, for which harsh penalties were provided in the articles, were desertion, cowardice and the concealing of loot 'to the value of even one piece of eight'. In the articles of Captain John Phillips, any pirate guilty of this last would be either shot or marooned. Of the two, shooting was preferable. Marooning meant putting a man ashore on a barren, uninhabited cay or reef and leaving him to die, making him, as the grim term was, 'the governor of an island'. Sometimes the culprit was given a pistol, powder and shot with which to end his misery when hunger and thirst became unbearable. It was a fiendish form of punishment and reflected the gravity of the crime, in pirate reckoning at least. Because of this custom pirates were known also as *marooners*.

An important article, observed punctiliously by the pirates in general, was that good quarter should be given to all who asked for it. This was simply a matter of sound policy. Pirates did not wish to fight unless they had to. If a ship offered no resistance, the custom was to treat the company, especially any women on board, well. It was a purely practical measure and had nothing to do with partiality towards one crew or another, for, as Bartholomew Roberts said: 'There is none of you but will hang me, I know, whenever you can clinch me within your power.' Resistance or the concealing of valuables were the unforgivable sins and punished mercilessly – another general policy which the pirates publicized, for good reason.

As with the buccaneers, a good deal has been written about the cruelty of the pirates. There were undoubtedly individual pirates conspicuous for their brutality, even in so harsh an age. Francis Spriggs was one, Edward Low another. On one occasion, having captured a French ship Low decided to burn her, first letting the crew go, except for the luckless cook who, it was felt 'being a greasy fellow would fry well in the fire', so he was lashed to the mast and burnt to death! The Calendar of State Papers records the case of certain pirates, predominantly British, who in October 1720 captured no less than sixteen French sloops off Dominica and Martinique, treating the crews with great cruelty and hanging the governor of Martinique who was on board one of them.

If a pirate company preferred a prize to their own ship they would give the prisoners the latter, or put them ashore at some suitable place if they wanted to keep both vessels. The crews of captured ships were usually given the chance of joining the pirates, an opportunity frequently grasped at. Pressing (or *forcing*) was seldom necessary, except in the case of skilled men, if they did not join of their own accord, such as carpenters, surgeons and sailing masters. Volunteers frequently asked discreetly to be given certificates to show that they had been forced, as a hedge in case they were captured and brought to trial. Judges were seldom deceived by this, however, and the plea was generally disallowed, as in the case of the piragua men who joined Jack Rackham in Negril Bay and were tried and condemned in the Jamaica Court of Vice-Admiralty.

Religion did not play an important part in the lives of the buccaneers or pirates, but even the wildest of them sometimes displayed a curious religious streak. Perhaps the strangest case of all was that of the then newly ordained graduate of Christ Church, Oxford, Lancelot Blackburne, one time minister of St Paul's, Falmouth, Antigua, later to become Archbishop of York, who roamed the Caribbean and Spanish Main with the buccaneers during 1681–82.

Captain Daniel, a French filibuster, combined a bloodthirsty piratical career with strict church discipline. The story is told that, sadly in need of provisions, Daniel anchored one night off one of the Saintes, a group of islets between Dominica and Guadeloupe, landed and seized the curé and certain other inhabitants, hauled them aboard his ship and informed them that all he needed was some fowls, brandy and wine. While these provisions were being hastily collected, Daniel thought it a good opportunity to have a celebration of the mass on board ship and the priest was prevailed upon to officiate.

All went well with the mass but for the insolence of one of the crew who 'remained in an indecent attitude' during the Elevation. A rebuke from his captain was answered by a fearful oath, whereupon Daniel whipped out his pistol and shot the offender through the head then tossed the body overboard so as not to delay proceedings. The curé's understandable alarm was allayed by Daniel who declared that the dead man was a rascal, lacking in his duty, 'and I have punished him to teach him better'.

Captain Sawkins permitted no gaming aboard his ship on the Sabbath, while it was concern at the lack of a Bible that forced Captain Phillips to have his articles sworn to on a hatchet! Among other things, that remarkable pirate Bartholomew Roberts was known for always going into action wearing a gold chain round his neck with a large diamond cross dangling from it. Himself a teetotaller he tried to enforce temperance aboard his ship as well as a proper respect for the sanctity of womanhood. He was a strict Sabbatarian and allowed the musicians on board to have a rest on the seventh day. This was a welcome relief, for the pirates had a right to demand a tune at any hour of day or night.

The fact is that piracy was grim and life at sea often deadly boring. Music helped relieve the tedium, as did dancing – a particularly favourite pastime – singing – an important cultural form for forging bonds among seamen – play-acting and mock trials at which each crewman took his turn at being judge and prisoner. This was a cynical form of pleasantry since there was always the possibility that each man would stand before a real judge in a real court of law.

'Good liquor to a sailor is preferable to clothing,' said Woodes Rogers; and gambling was a popular pastime which, however, often resulted in quarrels, fights and duels. Homosexuality was common and venereal diseases a problem. Ashore there were the brothels where casualties were probably higher than in battle, and the taverns where the searovers could 'melt the dollars', hard-earned at sword point and pistol, and forget for a while the tedium and basic pointlessness of their existence.

Charles Ellms in *The Pirate's Own Book* (1837) says, with admirable understatement, 'The pirate is truly fond of women and wine.' Of the two, wine, or more often hard liquor, was the greater weakness, perhaps because there was more opportunity to indulge in it. Some seamen believed that alcohol was healthful, especially in certain parts of the world, but for most drink offered a brief respite from the rigours of a hard life; it also served an important social function in the work culture of seafaring. As Johnson says, 'sobriety brought a man under suspicion of being in a plot against the Commonwealth and in that sense he was looked upon to be a villain that would not be drunk.'

Drink and its effects on their activities run like a connecting thread throughout the narratives. Prizes were lost and pirates captured because of drunkenness. Edward 'Blackbeard' Teach is pictured for us as a drunken braggart, and his grim practical jokes were usually played when he was 'a little flushed with drink'. Jack Rackham and his crew sometimes landed on a deserted cay to drink and carouse as long as their liquor lasted, then sailed away in search of more. He might not have been caught at Negril – a wild resort then as now – but for the fuddling effects of the rum punch he and his men had been swilling.

> O! Many a brave carouse I've known,
>   as many a seaman may,
> A-melting of the dollars with
>   the boys at Negril Bay.

But, behind it all, this heavy drinking probably took the place of something that was missing or lost, as drinking often does, and beneath the comradeship and the swagger, the oaths and the bowls of punch, was pathos and a sense of tragedy. The dream of the return home, for those who cherished it, grew dimmer with each voyage and each new day. As Robert Carse so well expresses it: 'Men heard in their heads the sound of Bow Bells that they were aware they would never really hear again; they imagined Devon meadows, a Breton orchard pink-white in the spring, or a Flemish windmill delicately traced upon the sky at dusk. More rum was the only answer.'

Speed was the chief consideration in pirate ships which, in general, were converted merchantmen, shallow in draught, long, lithe and low in the water. Pirates often raised the gunwales higher than normal, for breast-high gunwales gave more protection for the crew as well as a hiding place during a chase. Structural changes below decks included the removal of bulkheads, so that although every man had his own quarters for eating and sleeping, he should also have 'the same equality in ranging the ship all over'.

Pirates changed their ships as often as opportunity offered or need dictated. Size depended on the pirate's range. Thirty- to fifty-ton sloops were much favoured, but larger vessels were also used. Tonnage at this time was based on cubic capacity, not on weight of hull. Originally tonnage (or *tunnage*, as it was spelt) indicated the number of tuns (wine casks) a ship could carry. This calculation had its variations. Experienced sea captains had little difficulty in spotting a pirate craft, and a nerve-shaking experience each sighting must have been.

Weeds and barnacles, especially prevalent in the tropics, clinging to a ship's bottom made her slow and hard to steer. Since speed and manoeuverability were vital qualities in a pirate ship, it was necessary to clean her bottom often, every two or three months if possible, or at least three times a year. Marine borers, notably the teredo worm (a mollusc rather than a worm) were also a menace to wooden ships, except those made of fragrant, worm-resistant cedar. They entered the planking through tiny holes and channelled parallel to the surface. Reaching a length as adults of four to six inches, they could lay a million eggs a year and honeycomb a hull in short order. Other kinds of borer ate the ship's bottom from the outside. As protection ships were double-planked with a layer of felt and tar between, and cleaned frequently. The operation was known as *careening* (from the Latin word for 'keel'). First a suitably secluded bay or cove had to be found, preferably one with large trees growing down to the water's edge, and the ship run close in and beached. Guns and stores were removed, the top-mast was taken down and, with the aid of blocks and tackle, the ship was tilted over, first on one side and then on the other. Her bottom was scraped clean, repaired if necessary and coated with wax, tallow and tar, mixed sometimes with sulphur and arsenic.

Careening was a long and wearisome business, and dangerous too, as it laid a crew open to attack by some prowling, inquisitive man-of-war. As a precaution the ship's guns were usually mounted on improvised earthworks commanding the entrance to the bay, but many a pirate was taken, or forced to abandon his ship and escape inland, while careening. If time did not allow for a thorough job, a partial clean called 'boot-topping' was carried out.

The pirate flag was the *Jolly Roger* (a name of uncertain origin), known also simply as the Black Flag, or more pointedly – especially among the

Careening in a quiet cove

fraternity – as 'the Banner of King Death'. The traditional design was a white skull and crossed thigh bones on a black ground. This was an old symbol of mortality, commonly used in the gravestone art of the time, and was not peculiar to piracy. In fact, the pirates probably took the symbol from merchant captains who often drew the skull and crossed bones in the margins of their ships' logs to indicate the death of a crewman. Other popular designs included the skeleton (a 'human anatomy') holding a glass of punch in one hand and a sword in the other, a dart dripping blood, or an hourglass. The flag was intended to terrify the pirates' prey, of course, but, as Rediker points out, 'its triad of interlocking symbols – death, violence, limited time – simultaneously pointed to meaningful parts of the seaman's experience and eloquently bespoke the pirates' own consciousness of themselves as preyed upon in turn'.

Pirates sometimes fought under two flags, the black and a plain red. Reports suggest that the Jolly Roger was run up first to indicate an offer of quarter. If this was refused, the red or bloody flag was flown to signify that the offer had been withdrawn.

Stories of large amounts of treasure, buried by despotic pirate captains, are mainly myth, Robert Louis Stevenson notwithstanding. For one thing, pirate captains, as already explained, were not allowed to be despotic, and secondly, all booty had to be shared according to the rules. Few pirates amassed a fortune. They had neither the opportunity nor the inclination to do so. They had to trade their loot for cash and goods; they could not dine off doubloons, nor patch their ships' hulls with damask. The ambition of most was to make £700 to £800. Some achieved this goal and managed to retire. Captain John Evans' crew dispersed after a successful cruise with £300 each.

It is possible that some pirates hid part of their loot for safety and did not manage to recover it, but the buried treasure myth more probably springs from the stories put out by captured pirates – Kidd was one – in the hope of buying their acquittal. They were seldom believed.

Somewhere off the South American coast, at the bottom of the Pacific, lies the largest 'buried' treasure of all, awaiting a salvager: 699 pigs of silver, mistaken for tin by Bartholomew Sharp and his crew (during the venture in which Sawkins figured) found in the hold of a captured Spanish merchantman, the *Santo Rosario*, and discarded. One pig, kept by a crewman for casting into bullets, was later discovered to be solid silver by a jeweller in England. The cargo was worth more than £150,000!

General amnesties, known as Acts of Pardon or of Grace, or the King's Pardon, were frequently issued by Parliament in an effort to discourage

Pirate Flags

Jolly Roger, or Black Flag ~
the Banner of King Death

Jack Rackham

Pennant

Captain Bartholomew Roberts

A·B·H A·M·H

piracy, with mixed success. They were transmitted to the governors of the colonies who were empowered to accept surrenders within a stated period, and to issue certificates of pardon.

Many pirates surrendered under the acts, notably at New Providence in 1718 when Woodes Rogers went out as governor of the Bahamas, as well as in Jamaica and Bermuda, some intending genuinely to give up piracy for good and settle down to a life ashore, with a past wiped clean; but for most the Act of Grace was nothing more than a convenient breathing space. Abiding by the rules of the pardon would have meant a return to the wretched conditions from which they had escaped; besides, work was often difficult to come by since employers were frequently chary of engaging an ex-pirate. It has been suggested, in fact, that sometimes the amnesty proved to be an incentive to piracy, since wavering seamen were encouraged to 'go on the account' knowing they could leave the trade again, if they so wished, when the next act was passed. In general, these acts usually resulted in a division of piratical forces.

Pardon did not always follow surrender, however. Indeed, sometimes certain notorious pirates were specifically excluded, while various conditions under the acts often made for difficulties and even proved counter-productive, as in the case of John Williams, alias Yankee, and Jacob Everson, who claimed the King's Pardon at Montego Bay, Jamaica, in 1687. Yankee's ship was a large, Dutch-built affair with forty-four guns and a crew of a hundred, while Jacob's was a fine barque with a complement of fifty, mounting ten guns and sixteen patareros. (A patarero was a rather nasty little form of muzzle-loading mortar from which stones or rocks, broken glass, chain shot, old nails, scrap iron, etc. were fired.) The governor's reply to their offer of surrender proved disappointing. They were told they must break up their ships since, being foreign built, they could not be used for trade and consequently would find no buyers if sold. This was unacceptable to the pirates who weighed anchor and sailed out of port. As it happened, both were dead within a year.

An effective weapon in the fight against piracy was the establishment of Admiralty Courts in the American and West Indian colonies. Admiralty jurisdiction had existed in England from the thirteenth century and, with the era of colonial expansion, the need for jurisdiction of the kind overseas became evident. It was in Newfoundland, in 1615, that perhaps the earliest attempt to set up a court of vice-admiralty was made, principally as a result of fishing disputes. This did not prove very successful, but as governmental control over trade and colonization grew stronger, the idea spread to the North American continent and the Caribbean, and by the second half of the seventeenth century vice-admiralty courts had become a prominent feature of colonial life.

The first Act of Piracy was passed in the early part of the sixteenth century; the second and most important was that of William III in 1699 (renewed in Queen Anne's reign and later made perpetual) by which Courts of Admiralty set up in America were authorized to try all 'piracies, Felonies & Robberies committed in or upon the Sea or in any Haven, River, Creek or place', and to punish offenders on the spot.

In 1721 it was found necessary to pass another Piracy Act widening the scope of the earlier act considerably since, as it observed, 'The number of persons committing piracies upon the seas is of late much increased . . . notwithstanding the laws already made.' Later acts included those of 1744 and 1837, but by then the great age of piracy in the West Indies had ended.

This great age of piracy reached its peak in the first quarter of the eighteenth century, then vanished with dramatic suddenness. This is not to say that piracy itself ended then, if, in fact, it has ever really ceased, in other parts of the world at any rate. In the West Indies it was to drag on into the nineteenth century, until defeated by the weight of public opinion, the steam-engine and the telegraph.

The War of American Independence saw privateers swarming once more in the Caribbean, while the end, in 1815, of the long drawn-out hostilities between England and France brought into being a particularly unsavoury breed of pirates, lacking any of the humanity and romance of their predecessors. Spain, occupied with her rebellious South American colonies, could or would do nothing to help overcome this menace. In fact, Cuba acted at this time as an important clearing house, and Jamaica, in particular, found itself plagued by pirates operating out of secret creeks on Cuba's south coast. Many were captured, and once more on the brisk trade winds drifted the ominous groans of gibbet-chains on Jamaica's Gallows Point. In his book *Tom Cringle's Log*, Michael Scott vividly describes the simultaneous execution of twenty-five of these pirates. Eighteen others were hanged at the same place the following week, and for long afterwards this 'fearful and bloody example' struck terror into the Cuban pirates. This series of executions was the last of its kind and in time the monster gibbet at Gallows Point gradually rotted down and disappeared.

A number of factors contributed to the decline and eventual destruction of the 'real' piracy, as the West understood it. The 1721 Act of Piracy which encouraged merchant seamen to resist pirates probably played a part; that, and depriving the pirates of the bases from which to operate. In this connection, Captain Woodes Rogers who won and held the Bahamas against formidable odds, did as much as anyone to strangle piracy and bring its great epoch to an end. Rogers was famous in his own time for his remarkable privateering voyage around the world between 1708 and 1711, during which he sacked Guayaquil in Ecuador, and captured a number of prizes. The voyage was memorable also for the rescue of a Scottish seaman named Alexander Selkirk, marooned on Juan Fernández island, whose story furnished the source for Daniel Defoe's immortal *Robinson Crusoe*.

Stringent instructions to the colonial governors, that piracy was to be suppressed, and the support given to Britain's anti-piracy efforts, especially by the governors of Jamaica, Barbados, Virginia and Maryland, whose export trade stood to suffer most by the activities of the pirates, were also telling factors, as were the provision of more, bigger and better-manned warships and the more efficient and zealous policing of the seas by the Royal Navy.

These measures resulted in the capture and execution of a number of the more notorious pirates and their crews. In May 1722, forty-one men of a company of fifty-eight were taken in a single ship and hanged in Jamaica. In June the following year Finn, a well-known freebooter, was hanged in chains and five others were executed in Antigua, eleven more being hanged there nine months later. Some time earlier Jack Rackham and his famous women crew members, as well as Charles Vane, had been captured, and both men were hanged in Jamaica. It is estimated that between 1716 and 1726 as many perhaps as 600 Anglo-American pirates were executed. It was part of their pride that they walked 'to the gallows without a tear'.

For most it had been a short life but a merry one. As Bartholomew Roberts said, contrasting the horrors of 'honest service' with the pleasure and ease and liberty and power (and, one might add, with the 'honour' and 'justice' as they understood it) of the pirate way of life: 'Who', he asked, 'would not balance creditor on this side, when all the hazard that is run for it, at worst, is only a sour look or two at choking?'

Soon only the ungainly manatees rolled in the secret coves where the pirate sloops had lain on their sides at the careen, and the lumbering sea turtles left their trails in the soft sand of the secluded creeks where the crews had lain with their women, and drunk, and fought, and dared to live their own lives.

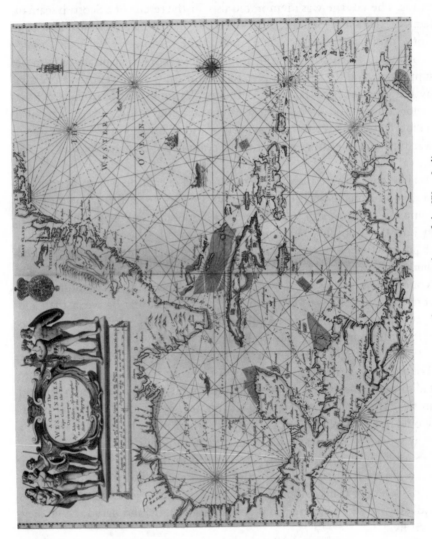

A late seventeenth-century chart of the West Indies

Henry Morgan

The great era of the buccaneers ended with the greatest of them all – Henry Morgan. In a sense the buccaneers were the forerunners of the West Indian pirates, although titles tended to shade into each other as the same man played different roles at different times.

More than three centuries have passed since Morgan first appeared on the scene, yet people still argue about the man, his role, his story and significance. *The Great Buccaneer*, one biographer calls him; *The Privateer*, another; *Pirate and Pioneer*, a third. He was all these and more besides – sailor of England, admiral and general, country gentleman and planter, runaway and bondsman, patriot and politician whose later career was to be crowned with a knighthood, the governorship of Jamaica and other official appointments including that of custos of his beloved Port Royal and judge of the Court of Vice-Admiralty. And yet that career started humbly enough.

Born about 1635, son of a Welsh land-owning farmer, perhaps the first West Indian island young Harry saw was Barbados – but under what auspices? As an ensign in the expeditionary force sent out in 1655 by Oliver Cromwell which captured Jamaica, as some declare, or as an indentured labourer 'bound . . . for three years to serve in Barbados', as others would have it – a version which Morgan hotly repudiated? He was in fact to win a famous libel action against the publishers of Esquemeling's book (one of the sources of this version) as a result of which it was publicly declared that 'he was a Gentleman's Son of good Quality in the County of Monmouth, and was never a Servant unto anybody in his life, unless unto his Majesty, the late King of England'. He was also cleared of any alleged 'cruelties and barbarous Usages of the Spaniards when at his Mercy or his Prisoners', but that is another matter. Morgan once said in writing to the Lords of Trade and Plantations (forerunners of the Colonial Office), 'I left the schools too young to be a great proficient in either that [Admiralty] or other laws, and have been much more used to the pike than the book.' The fact is that great

Henry Morgan as a young man

men often have no beginnings. Morgan swept into the Caribbean like a hurricane, as one biographer puts it, apparently coming from nowhere and then disappearing almost without a trace, which is only partly true – and this, anyway, is to run ahead of our narrative.

Making his way from Barbados to Tortuga, Morgan joined the Brethren of the Coast, taking part in a number of notable raids along the coasts of South America and sailing in search of prizes at sea, learning his trade – 'the sweet trade', it was called – like any other ambitious apprentice. He became a member of Edward Mansfield's crew and later, on the old chief's death in 1667, its acclaimed leader. The governor of Jamaica, Sir Thomas Modyford, had employed Mansfield, issuing him *Letters of Marque* (privateer commissions) against Spain, this being, as he pointed out to his superiors in England, the only way of keeping the buccaneers from becoming the enemies of Jamaica. He was prepared to use Morgan in the same way. In Welsh Harry, in fact, he was to find his strongest ally: the ruthless, resourceful buccaneer leader who could hold the wild Brethren together and direct their main efforts towards the defence of the island.

But Morgan was more than a buccaneer captain. The same man who could swear and curse and drink and whore with the best of them in many a den of murder, or lead a bunch of desperadoes for miles through hostile jungles and fever-ridden swamps, up treacherous rivers and along dangerous coasts, was also to prove an astute politician with a breadth of vision far, far beyond that of the men he drew to him with his rare magnetism. It is no wonder that he and Modyford, the barrister and shrewd administrator, were to become firm friends and close conspirators.

Morgan's first important exploit in his new role was the sacking of Puerto Príncipe (now Camagüey) in Cuba in 1668. Modyford had commissioned him 'to take prisoners of the Spanish nation' in order to discover if it were true that the Spaniards intended to attack Jamaica. The people of the town, who had been warned of the approaching force, moved their valuables out and prepared to resist the attack, surrendering only after a bloody house-to-house battle. Under torture some disclosed the hiding places of their valuable possessions. The buccaneers also scoured the countryside and collected large quantities of raw goods, but not much gold or silver. While waiting for the ransom money he had demanded, Morgan discovered that the emissaries he had sent were only temporizing, until the governor of Santiago, then on his way to Puerto Príncipe with a large force, should come to their rescue. Cutting his losses, Morgan altered the levy from cash to 500 oxen, to be driven to the shore, slaughtered, and the meat salted and loaded on his ships. He then weighed anchor and sailed away.

The Towne of Puerto del Principe taken & sackt

Part 2: Cha

The sacking of Puerto Príncipe (Camagüey) by pirates

Incidentally, he claimed to have had confirmation of the Spanish plans to attack Jamaica, which, of course, was the purpose of the action. So Morgan at least was satisfied, but not his men: the *purchase* when shared among the company was so small that it would not pay their debts in Jamaica. This probably suited the Welshman. As long as his men were hungry for gold he could entice them back to work, and for his next project – a raid on Porto Bello – they would need strong enticement.

Situated on the Caribbean end of the trade route across the Isthmus of Panama, Porto Bello was the third strongest city in the Indies. It was also one of the wealthiest, and Morgan stressed this fact, promising his followers rich gain as the prize for success. The harbour of the beautiful port was deep enough to take the largest galleon, but its entrance was protected by two formidable castles, while on a tall cliff behind the town rose the great fortress of San Jeronimo. An open attack from the sea would have been madness, but Morgan had other ideas: he proposed to steal on the city from behind. Unconvinced, the French members of the force defected to a man, but this did not discourage the great buccaneer. Appealing to the bravery and greed of his remaining followers, Morgan pointed out in a stirring speech that if their numbers were small their hearts were great, and the fewer they were the better shares they would have in the spoils. The speech had a magical effect and his confidence was rewarded. With masterful if brutal tactics and brave fighting, he captured the city. A relieving force sent from Panama was ambushed by the buccaneers and cut to pieces.

While Morgan was at Porto Bello the governor of Panama, Don Juan Pérez de Guzmán, sent a sarcastic message to him, asking for some small pattern of the arms with which he had taken with such violence so great a city. Morgan treated the messenger with much civility, and gave him a pistol and a handful of shot to take back to the governor, with the promise that he would fetch them away himself within a twelvemonth. His Excellency, says the story, made haste to return the pistol with grateful thanks and, sending a gold ring set with a fine emerald as a gift, entreated Captain Morgan not to give himself the trouble of coming to Panama as he would not speed so well there as he had done at Porto Bello. But Morgan was not long in keeping his promise.

The buccaneers sailed from Porto Bello, possibly to their favourite meeting place, a small rocky cay off the south-western end of Hispaniola called Ile-à-Vache, 'Cow Island', a name which the English corrupted to Isle of Ash. Here the vast loot of gold and silver, jewels, rich silks and other valuables, as well as some 300 black slaves, estimated to have been worth 250,000 pieces-of-eight, was divided according to the rules, the King and Modyford getting their share and Morgan his five percent.

Back in Jamaica, Morgan wrote his brief official report of the action, leaving out most of the unpleasant details, but making much of the fact that he had released eleven Englishmen from Porto Bello dungeons. Modyford was a little alarmed by the raid, for Morgan's commission empowered him to attack shipping only! But there was not much he could do, or probably wished to do, besides express his formal disapproval.

Soon Morgan was on the move again, clutching another commission from Modyford. Once more he and his fleet sailed to their rendezvous at Ile-à-Vache where this time Morgan very nearly lost his life. It was New Year's Day, the year 1669, and Welsh Harry had hoisted his flag on his new acquisition, the *Oxford*, a Royal frigate sent to him by Modyford, and summoned his captains to a council to hear what he proposed – an attack on the 'Pearl of the Indies' no less, the great fortified city of Cartagena.

Situated on the Caribbean coast of what is now the Republic of Colombia, Cartagena, together with Porto Bello, handled the treasure that came up the Pacific side from Chile, Peru and Ecuador, to Panama. Snug behind its great bays, ringed with forts, notably the enormous castle of San Felipe, Cartagena was by far the most powerful harbour on the Main. Despite the dangers involved, however, Morgan's proposal found favour with his captains, and a delighted Harry, always game for a carouse, invited everyone to stay aboard for dinner.

Then the drinking started for joy of their new voyage, 'in testimony whereof', wrote one of their number, 'they drank many healths and discharged many guns, as is the common sign of mirth among seamen.' But the frigate's gunner had become negligent and something went wrong. At the height of the celebration there was a blinding flash and deafening roar as the *Oxford*'s magazine blew up, ripping the vessel apart. All the captains sitting opposite Morgan at the table in the great cabin were killed instantly, while he and those on his side were blown out of the ship and into the sea, unharmed! By dawn Morgan and the survivors were picked up by the other ships' boats, but 250 of those aboard the *Oxford* – all but six men and four cabin boys – had perished in the blast. The loss of the frigate was compensated for by the seizure of a fine French ship present at the time, *Le Cerf Volant*, which Morgan sent back to Modyford. She was later to be renamed *The Satisfaction* and become Harry's flagship.

The loss of so many seasoned buccaneers and experienced captains, however, now made the attack on Cartagena impractical and the destination was eventually changed to Maracaibo, an important seaport in Venezuela, on the west shore of the strait joining lake and gulf, sacked by L'Olonnais two years before.

The approaches to Maracaibo were difficult and dangerous. The gulf passed, there remained the narrow strait, guarded by an earthwork and a fort built since L'Olonnais' raid, to be negotiated. The advance was costly, but by the time the buccaneers successfully rushed the fort the Spanish defenders had deserted it, leaving behind a sinister silence and a booby trap designed to destroy both fortress and invaders, which Morgan's catlike sense of danger soon detected. In one of the dark, cutstone chambers he found a powder train, set to burn for fifteen minutes, sputtering and glowing in the light wind with only five of those minutes to go. In one swift movement Morgan ripped the length of hemp cord free and stamped out its burning end!

He now passed on to Maracaibo, and later to Gibraltar at the head of the lake, where he and his men spent weeks in an orgy of drinking, merry-making and torturing the wretched inhabitants to induce them to give up their gold and precious stuff.

But Morgan had lingered too long in the lake. He returned to find his exit through the strait blocked by three powerful Spanish galleons. From this point the Maracaibo expedition gains in interest and dignity. There was a long military tradition in the Morgan family and Harry's intentions were always concerned with the land. He was at heart a soldier and only incidentally a sailor. On this occasion the naval and military skill he displayed and the craft and courage by which he bluffed, forced and fought his way to the open sea and to safety marked him as a strategist of the highest order.

The Spanish *flota* was commanded by Vice-Admiral Alonso del Campo y Espinosa who smirked with satisfaction from the castle of his flagship, the forty-eight-gun *Magdalen*, at the buccaneer's plight. But Morgan was equal to the challenge. With characteristic cheek he sent the admiral a message demanding a considerable sum as the price for not burning Maracaibo to the ground, and, presumably, safe conduct for his ships! The admiral's reply was firm and to the point: 'My intent is to dispute with you your passage out of the Lake, and follow and pursue you everywhere.' He did add shrewdly that if Morgan surrendered everything he had taken, including prisoners, he would let him pass freely. Morgan of course did not trust the assurance, and nor did his men – when he put it to them in council – who answered with one voice that they would rather fight to the death than surrender any of the booty they had gained.

Morgan now sprang the most ingenious stratagem of his career. He had a *brûlot*, or fireship, prepared, loaded with sulphur, pitch, tar and quantities of black powder, with fuses set ready for the lighting. Wooden imitation guns lined the deck and glared menacingly from the ports, while lifelike dummies dressed as crewmen stood all about. Twelve buccaneers volunteered for the suicide mission of sailing the fireship into the Spanish fleet and, grappling the nearest ship, set her alight. The second galleon with the admiral aboard ran towards the fort and was scuttled, while the third was captured by Morgan. So ended the naval phase of the operation: Harry now faced the task of getting past the reinforced fort, commanded by a furious Don Alonso.

The device Morgan used was an old trick of warfare. He spent a whole day ferrying boatloads of his men to land, to a point at the rear of the fort. This part of the operation was carried out in full view of the enemy watching from the walls, but what they did not see was that, once among the mangroves, all the buccaneers, except the oarsmen, huddled down low in the boats as they returned to the ships, the operation being repeated until it seemed to the Spaniards that hundreds of men had been ferried ashore, whereas the ruse had been practised by the same handful of men. Assuming that Morgan's intention was to attempt the walls of the fort, Don Alonso had all the heavy artillery laboriously turned to the land side, leaving the strait-facing bastions almost totally undefended.

Roaring with laughter, Morgan led his fleet that night by moonlight out of the lake, firing a defiant salvo at the fort as he passed by.

With flags flying gaily and gunfire stirring echoes from the lush and lofty Blue Mountains across the splendid harbour, Morgan and his Brethren sailed into their base at old Port Royal with loot said to have amounted to a quarter of a million pieces-of-eight, to be joyously greeted by all – except the governor. Dispatches had begun to arrive from London expressing the King's displeasure over the Porto Bello raid and holding Modyford answerable for it. Morgan was again reprimanded and his commission temporarily withdrawn. He was also advised to leave Port Royal for the present – a harsh blow for the wild Welshman who loved the gay and noisy life of the wicked port. All the same he knew full well the reasons for Modyford's action, and so retired discreetly to his country property and the company of Mary Elizabeth his wife.

It was probably some time in 1666 that Morgan, then about 30 years old and already rich from the proceeds of profitable buccaneering expeditions, had married his first cousin Mary Elizabeth, daughter of General Edward Morgan and his well-born wife, herself the daughter of a Saxon nobleman the Baron von Polnitz. The old general had preceded Modyford as deputy-governor of the island in 1664, and briefly held the post of lieutenant-governor, under Sir Thomas, until his death the following year.

Henry's marriage brought him at once into direct relationship with Colonel Robert Byndloss, the husband of his wife's eldest sister Anna Petronella, and, later, with Colonel Henry Archbould who married another sister, Joanna Wilhelmina. Byndloss and Archbould were both members of the Council and men of considerable influence in the island.

Although they produced no children, Henry and Mary seem to have had a happy enough married life, despite Harry's many absences and his dangerous and profligate way of living. They mixed with the planter families on equal terms and were frequent visitors to the King's House. Over the years Morgan increased his Jamaican property holdings considerably, with the purchase of Danks and what came to be called Morgan's Valley in Clarendon, of Llanrhumny in St Mary, of 4,000 acres near Lucea in the distant parish of Hanover, and Lawrencefield near Port Henderson where it is believed he died.

But to return to Modyford: soon he could write to his superiors in London that all was peace and quiet in the island, and that most of the buccaneers, like Henry Morgan himself, had become planters or merchants. But it was an uneasy peace, broken in the early part of 1670 by Spanish attacks on English shipping and a raid on Jamaica's north coast by a man-of-war, during which plantations were burnt and the owners and their slaves carried off.

Once more invasion rumours began to circulate and tempers to grow hot, chiefly among the Brethren of the Coast at Port Royal, especially when a boastful Spanish captain named Manuel Rivera Pardal landed near Negril at the island's western end. He nailed a placard to a tree claiming that he had attacked English shipping and raided English territory, including the Cayman Islands where he burnt twenty houses, and challenging Morgan to 'come out upon the coast and seek me, that he might see the valour of the Spaniards'.

The boasts of the vapouring Spanish captain were of relative unimportance to Morgan or Modyford: what mattered far more was the excuse they gave for official action. As it happened, two months later one of Morgan's most trusted captains, John Morris, driven by strong winds into a bay off the east of Cuba, fell in with the boastful Rivera Pardal aboard his man-of-war, attacked and killed him.

On 29th June 1670, Modyford called a meeting of the Council to consider what action should be taken. It was decided to commission Morgan once more, but now as 'Admiral and Commander-in-Chief of all the ships of war belonging to this harbour', with instructions not only to destroy Spanish vessels, but also 'to land in the enemy's country as many of his men as he shall judge needful . . . and finally to do all manner of exploits which may tend to the preservation and quiet of this island, being his Majesty's chief interest in the Indies.' This was precisely what the buccaneer wished: it opened the way for an attack on Panama City which he had been meditating for some time – his greatest and most daring exploit, and his last.

Morgan sailed to beautiful Bluefields Bay on Jamaica's south-west coast for a rendezvous with his fleet. From the deck of his flagship he would have looked across at the great rampart of the Bluefields Ridge, rising half a mile into the clouds in one conical peak, then running out into the Bay as a bold promontory covered to the very edge of the beach with dense, primeval forest, while overhead the watchful frigate birds wheeled in graceful, effortless flight.

With his fleet of thirty-six ships now assembled, Morgan sailed eastwards for Ile-à-Vache from which, in December, announcing that the taking of Panama stood most for the good and safety of Jamaica, he set sail. The island of Old Providence, off the coast of Nicaragua (not to be confused with New Providence in the Bahamas), a favourite buccaneer haunt about three-quarters of the way from Jamaica to the Main, was captured en route and used as an advance base for the attack on the strongly fortified town of Chagres on the Caribbean side of the Isthmus. The path to Panama was now open and Morgan with some 1,200 men began his historic march on the city.

For more than eight days they stumbled forward, hacking a way through the thick jungle, scorched at times by the blazing sun, then drenched by sudden tropical showers of rain, tormented by flies and mosquitoes and harassed by stealthy Indians who shot their flights of arrows and vanished before a pistol could be cocked. The buccaneers had reckoned on living off the country and so carried almost no provisions, but the Spaniards, warned of their coming, had stripped the land bare of everything that could be safely eaten. To the other hardships then was added that of hunger which, as the days went by, became so intense that at one stage the buccaneers were reduced to eating leather bags – softened in water, cut into strips and roasted – for food. Only Morgan's iron will and matchless leadership held the ragged, bearded, hunger-maddened men together and drove them relentlessly towards their glittering goal which they first glimpsed with joy on the evening of the ninth day.

Among Spain's New World cities Panama stood supreme. Besides the royal houses – the governor's palace with its cool, tiled patios and richly mirrored chambers, the law courts and the treasury filled with gold and silver from Peru and Potosí – there were 2,000 merchants' homes and 5,000 more belonging to tradesmen and people of lesser degree, as well as numerous chapels, monasteries and convents, many with fine towers: so high in fact was the tower of the cathedral that the Indians believed the angels reached out from heaven to ring the bells.

On the plains before the city the ragged buccaneers were met by a force of immaculate Spanish cavalry and foot soldiers, supported by artillery and led by the old governor, which outnumbered them three to one. Steadily the tattered flags of the rabble army advanced across the plains and a furious pitched battle was joined – Morgan's first fight on an open battlefield – which he soon turned to advantage by a masterful outflanking of the enemy.

At this point the governor sprang his great surprise. Two herds of bulls and oxen numbering 1,500 each were stampeded into the right and left angles of the attackers' rear. But you did not frighten buccaneers with bulls: they had slaughtered them for a living in the forests of Hispaniola. Some well-aimed shots by buccaneer marksmen soon worked panic in the herds which, wheeling around, trampled the herdsmen to death and helped throw the Spanish forces into disorder. On the heels of the bellowing bulls came the wildly cheering buccaneers, and Panama was doomed. The Spanish survivors fled back to the city, but in a few hours all resistance was crushed.

Victory was followed by an orgy of looting, torturing and wild celebration. Esquemeling tells of scores of women being raped, and weaves a highly romantic story around the surpassingly beautiful 'Lady of Panama' who would have preferred death to dishonour at the hands of Morgan. But the expedition's surgeon-general, Richard Browne, writing some months after the Panama raid, at a time when he was enraged with Morgan, could still say, 'as to their women I know nor ever heard of anything offered beyond their wills,' adding that the Admiral was noble enough to the vanquished enemy.

At the height of the sack a fire started, caused possibly by the blowing up of the powder magazine at the governor's orders, which was to reduce the place to ashes. 'Thus', reported Morgan, 'was consumed the famous and ancient city of Panama.'

Morgan stayed twenty days in Panama, making daily incursions for miles around and taking prisoners. One of the chief prizes, La Santissima Trinidad, laden with all the gold, silver and jewels the government and rich citizens had managed to ship out of the city, escaped his grasp because the men who should have taken her were too drunk to stir.

In February 1671 the buccaneer party started on the return journey with 175 pack-animals laden with the loot – gold and silver, jewellery and precious stones, treasure from the churches, rich vestments, plate, ornaments and other costly stuff – as well as 600 captives. Most of the prisoners were sold and the rest ransomed later, bringing the total value of the Panama plunder to 750,000 pieces-of-eight, but after all the heavy deductions were made, each buccaneer received 200 pieces-of-eight only, or rather less than £50.

Esquemeling says that feeling among the men began to run against Morgan, perhaps because of the smallness of the *purchase*. Some writers claim he cheated his men; others refute this, but the stigma stuck:

> For diddling of old shipmates,
> For cutting with the pay,
> I'd like to see 'is equal –
> It were not Lollonais!*

We shall probably never know the full answer.

Another reproach levelled at Morgan by Esquemeling is that he abandoned his men at the end, boarding his ship secretly and sailing for Jamaica accompanied by only three or four vessels of the whole fleet. But, say the Morgan advocates, this implication of desertion is preposterous. The division of plunder was openly conducted and the men paid off. The expeditionary force would then have considered itself disbanded with all units free to go where they pleased.

An uproarious reception greeted Morgan's return to Port Royal, including a formal vote of thanks from the Council for the manner in which he had carried out his commission, but this time the buccaneer and governor had gone too far. In July 1670 the Treaty of Madrid had been signed, sealing peace between Spain and England and acknowledging the latter's right to hold American colonies, including Jamaica. Modyford did not know of this until Morgan had sailed. It is possible that he could have recalled the buccaneer before the landing on the Isthmus. Perhaps he tried. On the other hand, both men may have decided to deliver the final blow to Spain's might in the Caribbean, whatever the consequences . . . and these were to follow swiftly after the news of Panama reached Europe.

Spain's ambassador protested strongly and demanded satisfaction. Some action had to be taken. Accordingly, in June 1671, Sir Thomas Lynch came

* E. H. Visiak, 1910 *Buccaneer Ballads*

out to replace Modyford as governor and to send him as a prisoner to England where, on arrival, he was shut up in the Tower of London. Morgan followed in April of the following year, to answer for his part in breaking the Treaty of Madrid. The recall of both men, however, was little more than a sop to Spain's hurt pride: Sir Thomas lived in ease and comfort while in prison and the great buccaneer was entertained as a hero in London, spending riotous nights in the company of rakish young nobles, including the Duke of Albemarle who was later to be appointed governor of Jamaica.

Eventually the two daring and far-sighted friends were cleared of all disgrace, and, by a surprising change in policy, Morgan was knighted and made lieutenant-governor of the island, King Charles expressing 'particular confidence in his loyalty, prudence, and courage, and long experience of that colony'. Modyford was rewarded with the post of Chief Justice, and so were the two friends reunited. On his tombstone in the Cathedral, Spanish Town, Modyford is described as 'The Soule and Life of all Jamaica who first made it what it now is.'

Like the great buccaneer himself, Port Royal was now at its zenith, and for both the end was not far distant. From city fortress, to trading centre and slave depot, to headquarters of the dread Brethren under Harry's inspired leadership, were short easy steps, and by its heyday the old port had earned the title of the world's richest and wickedest city.

Warehouses lined the waterfront, packed with choice merchandise. Life might have been cheap, but house rentals were high, as high in fact as in London's most fashionable sections. Taverns had proliferated to the point where there was one to every ten residents. Prostitutes abounded, for here they could be 'wicked without shame and whore on without punishment'. Goldsmiths and silversmiths had more work than they could handle, for every householder kept a cupboard of rich plate which he 'carelessly exposed . . . being in no apprehension of Thieves for want of receivers'. There were faiths of every kind, from papist to atheist, and churches of most denominations, but the clergy despaired of saving souls, succeeding only, in the words of the Anglican rector of the time, in keeping up some show of religion among a most ungodly and debauched people.

To its fine, sheltered harbour came the deep-freighted merchantmen and men-of-war, the packets and the slavers, their human cargoes shackled below 'with not so much room as a man in his coffin'. Here came the buccaneer sloops, laden with Spanish spoil. Ashore their seamen swaggered along the narrow, sandy streets – Lime Street and Thames Street, Cannon, Broad and Tower Streets – to brothel and tavern, their pockets bulging with jewellery and gleaming doubloons soon to find their way into the purses of sharp-eyed strumpets and the coffers of fat merchants.

But the heyday of buccaneering was fast drawing to a close. To the merchants and some of the big proprietors it had brought wealth, but with the increasing agricultural development of the country, the powerful planting interest began to look with distaste on buccaneering, especially because it lured men away in droves from agricultural work. Meanwhile, as the stage was being set for the new policy of attracting the trade of the Spanish Indies into English hands, with Jamaica as one of the principal entrepôts, the interference of the buccaneers became undesirable. The fact is that by removing the threat of Spain so effectively, the old filibusters had worked themselves out of a job. Many failed to grasp this and ended with a noose around their necks at Gallows Point, a promontory to the east of Port Royal – often on Morgan's orders – because they would not give up their old way of life.

The retired buccaneer himself, at the age of 53, was sick and old beyond his years, 'much given to drinking and sitting up late'. Albemarle's private physician, Sir Hans Sloane, who attended Sir Henry shortly before he died, found him lean, sallow-coloured, his stomach jutting out. He and a local black doctor to whom Morgan resorted, did their best for their patient, but on 25th August 1688, he died, probably from tuberculosis, and was buried in the cemetery on the sea-beaten Palisadoes, as the guns of Fort Charles and those of all the ships in the harbour thundered a last salute. Four years later, on 7th June 1692, a devastating earthquake plunged the better part of the old port beneath the harbour, taking the cemetery and Morgan's grave with it. The sea had claimed her own.

Sir Thomas Lynch, governor of Jamaica from 1671 to 1675, was ruthless in suppressing the buccaneers. 'This cursed trade', he once exclaimed, 'has been so long followed, and there is so many of it that like weeds or hydras they spring up as fast as we can cut them down.' Although his successors Lord Vaughan and the Earl of Carlisle, and later the Duke of Albemarle, were a little less strict, the day of the Jamaican buccaneer at least was at an end. Proclamations offering free pardons to those who would give up 'the sweet trade' and settle down as peaceful citizens had some effect, but many of the more confirmed searovers preferred to stick to buccaneering, in spite of the threats of dire punishment if caught.

The sack of Panama by Morgan had stirred the imagination of many of the Brethren. This, coupled with the anti-buccaneering spirit abroad in the Caribbean, caused some of the bolder hearts to turn their thoughts to the Pacific Ocean and the riches still to be garnered from the undefended cities along the coast. 'This inspiration led to the second era, in which the buccaneers reached their greatest height of daring, prosperity and power,' writes Philip Gosse – the era of the Pacific ventures.

In 1679 a group of English and French buccaneers launched the first large-scale operation since the days of Henry Morgan when they attacked Porto Bello, took it and withdrew without loss. A year later a far more ambitious expedition was planned: this was to march across the Isthmus of Darien to Panama, sack the city, then embark on a piratical cruise into the Pacific, returning home by way of Cape Horn.

A number of famous buccaneer captains took part, some of them men of good birth and education, five of whom wrote journals of the expedition, including the naturalist William Dampier, the surgeon Lionel Wafer, and Basil Ringrose whose account is perhaps the best of the lot, making this most remarkable buccaneering expedition one of the best documented.

To follow its course is outside the scope of this work, but the part played in its early stages by one of the captains, Richard Sawkins, will typify that of the men who stood out in this era of buccaneering.

Captain Richard Sawkins

As with so many of these searovers, nothing seems to be known of Sawkins' origins and little of his early career. He figures in a letter dated 1st December 1679 from the Earl of Carlisle, then governor of Jamaica, to the Secretary of State in London, advising that Captain Thomas Johnson of HMS *Success* had taken one Captain Sawkins with his vessel, suspected of being a privateer, and had sent him in to Port Royal where he was in the custody of the provost marshal, awaiting trial.

The *Success* meanwhile, chasing another buccaneer, among the South Cays of Cuba, named Peter Harris (he was to play a prominent role in the Pacific Venture), 'bilged upon her anchor and became irrecoverable' – in other words, hopelessly holed. In the end, only her guns, sails and anchors could be salvaged.

When news of the mishap was received, Carlisle promptly ordered Sawkins' brigantine to the South Cays, commanded by a lieutenant of the *Success*, with sundry members of the ship's company, and fresh water and food for the crewmen still in the stricken warship. Equally promptly Sawkins contrived to escape from gaol by night, get hold of a wherry and, steering after his brigantine, which was becalmed before she was to leeward of the island, overtook, boarded and carried her, putting to sea with thirty-six men!

Shortly after recovering his vessel Sawkins sighted a sail, chased and overhauled it. It proved to be 'a great Spanish Shipp . . . well fleshed with 150 men', but young Sawkins – who was to go down in buccaneer annals as 'a man whom nothing could terrifie' – succeeded in boarding her, withdrawing only after a fierce hand-to-hand fight which cost the Spaniard thirty men killed or wounded.

Sawkins lost ten of his own small crew in the bloody engagement, including the lieutenant of the *Success*. He was to even the score with the Spaniards in time, but for the present there was the sad business of seeing to his own dead comrades. Standing in for the leeward part of the island he hove to and anchored as close as he could. It was a melancholy procession that made its way up the wet, grey sands of the deserted beach to a now unknown, secluded spot at the edge of the forest, where the ten brave crew members were buried. Sawkins, no cynical atheist, probably presided over a brief service for the dead. It is recorded of him that one Sunday morning, finding some of his men gambling, he seized the dice and threw it into the sea, saying that he would have no gambling aboard his ship on the Sabbath.

Refitting the brigantine and drumming up recruits along the coast, Sawkins was spotted by HMS *Hunter*, prowling in the area at the time. The warship's captain immediately manned out his pinnace to inquire into the brigantine's presence, but it was an angry Sawkins who, warning them not to attempt to board, saw them off with a volley of small shot. The *Hunter* then sent in a sloop which she had in company, to engage the buccaneers, but in the last official reference to the matter we read that 'of the issue, as yet His Excellency hath no certain accompt'. If he ever learnt what happened on that lee shore, as, of course, he certainly must have, the records are eloquently silent. The fact is that Sawkins escaped the *Hunter*'s toils, and there is no suggestion that her captain was reprimanded for this. The loss of HMS *Success* was a far more serious matter, the blame for which fell on the luckless pilot, who was court martialled in February 1680 and sentenced to be whipped aboard five several ships on three days, one after the other, to be imprisoned for a year, and forbidden from ever piloting a King's ship again. He probably did not survive the floggings.

As for the provost marshal from whose custody Sawkins escaped – and whom the governor had resolved to handle 'very severely' – nothing further is heard, which suggests that his role in the mortifying incident was discreetly forgotten. The Earl of Carlisle himself, after a somewhat frustrating governorship, returned to England where he died in 1685 and was buried in York Minster with great pomp befitting so distinguished a nobleman.

Sawkins lost no time in making contact with other Brethren of the Coast and we next hear of him at Bocas del Toro, a popular buccaneer careening place, throwing in his lot with the leaders of the Darien Venture – Captains John Coxon and Bartholomew Sharp. His contribution was small: his old 16-ton brigantine manned by 35 men and mounting one gun only. Coxon, on the other hand, commanded a 60-tonner of 8 guns and 97 men, while Peter Harris' ship of 150 tons, the largest in the fleet, boasted 25 guns and a complement of 107 men.

After refitting and taking on supplies, the party of 331 buccaneers landed on the Darien Coast on 5th April 1680 and began their march through the jungle towards the Pacific. The Darien Indians had a longstanding feud with the Spaniards and many of them, including two chiefs, joined the buccaneers as confederates, supplying them with meat and fruit in exchange for knives, axes, beads and other trade truck. The Indians urged the buccaneers to attack the town of Santa Maria which lay on the route, being, as they said, the place from which the gold mined in the surrounding mountains was transported to Panama.

The company was divided into eight divisions, each led by a buccaneer captain with his own distinguishing flag, Sawkins' being red striped with yellow. In the marching order Bartholomew Sharp, still weak from a bout of illness, led the first company with Sawkins leading the second.

The journey, which involved marching in difficult terrain, wading waist-deep through winding, fast-flowing rivers and man-handling the canoes over rocks as well as trees felled by the Spaniards to impede their progress, was a wearisome and tedious one and probably accounted in part for the first of the clashes between the company commanders which were to plague the expedition. The hot-tempered Coxon, jealous of Sawkins' popularity with the men, picked a quarrel with him, then later had some disagreement with Harris during which he fired his musket at him. Harris was about to fire in return when some of the buccaneers intervened and eventually they patched up the quarrel.

Santa Maria proved to be poorly protected by a simple palisade which the buccaneers easily breached. So fierce was their onslaught, however, that twenty-six Spaniards were killed and sixteen wounded in the brief action.

But the results were disappointing. Warned of their approach, the Spaniards had spirited away almost everything of value and, according to one of the buccaneers, 'though we examined our prisoners severely', the total spoil amounted only to 20 pounds weight of gold and a small quantity of silver, whereas three days earlier they would have found 300 pounds of gold in the fort alone! Disappointment with the Santa Maria venture led to another crisis of command which was only settled by Coxon's being named leader.

The adventurers then proceeded downriver in their canoes, entering the Bay of Panama on 19th April where they took a 30-ton Spanish ship to which 130 of them transferred, glad to be rid of the cramped and crowded conditions of the canoes. On the 22nd they set off for Panama, coming in sight of the city the following morning, being the 'Day of St George, our Patron of England'.

This was the new city, built about four miles west of the one destroyed by Henry Morgan. It was considerably bigger than the old and as yet largely unfinished. The churches, eight in number, were under construction, and the old cathedral was still being used, making, according to Ringrose, 'a fair show at a distance, like unto the Church of St Paul's at London'.

As the buccaneers approached the city three Spanish men-of-war sailed out to the attack. Unfortunately the buccaneers had sent away the barque, captured earlier, with over 100 of their best men, in search of water, so they had only the canoes with which to engage the warships.

The fierce fighting that followed lasted almost the whole day. The Spaniards fought bravely, but lost heart when Sawkins, after being repulsed three times, succeeded in boarding one of the warships. A second soon fell to the buccaneers while the third made off as fast as she could. The Spanish commander and a large number of his men were killed, while of the buccaneers, eighteen died and some thirty were wounded, including Captain Harris who was shot in both legs and died two days later of his wounds.

This was Sawkins' finest action. His inspired leadership and dauntless courage were chiefly responsible for the victory. It also won him the confidence and deep respect of the buccaneers who, on the other hand, were openly critical of Coxon's cowardly conduct during the fight. As a result, Coxon decided to abandon the Pacific venture and return across the Isthmus with some of his followers. He eventually made his way to Jamaica. With his departure young Sawkins was unanimously chosen 'general and chief commander'.

The buccaneers now stood towards Panama, but not considering their strength sufficient for a siege contented themselves with blockading the harbour, seizing the ships they found anchored there and any others that unwisely strayed into the neighbourhood. One of these, *La Santissima Trinidad* of 400 tons, had a considerable sum of money on board, as well as jars of wine, brandy, sugar and sweetmeats. In other prizes, which they added to their fleet, they found flour and ammunition, gunpowder, iron, skins, soap and a cargo of African slaves which so tempted the less scrupulous Spanish merchants that many carried on a clandestine night-time trade with the buccaneers.

It was during these exchanges that the governor of Panama sent Sawkins a message demanding to know why, during a time of peace between England and Spain, they should come into those seas to do them injury, and from whom they had their commissions; to which Sawkins replied, characteristically, that 'he and his companions came to assist their friend the king of Darien, who was the rightful lord of Panama, and all the country thereabouts. That as they had come so far it was reasonable they should receive some satisfaction for their trouble; and, if the governor would send them 500 pieces of eight for each man, and 1000 for each commander, and

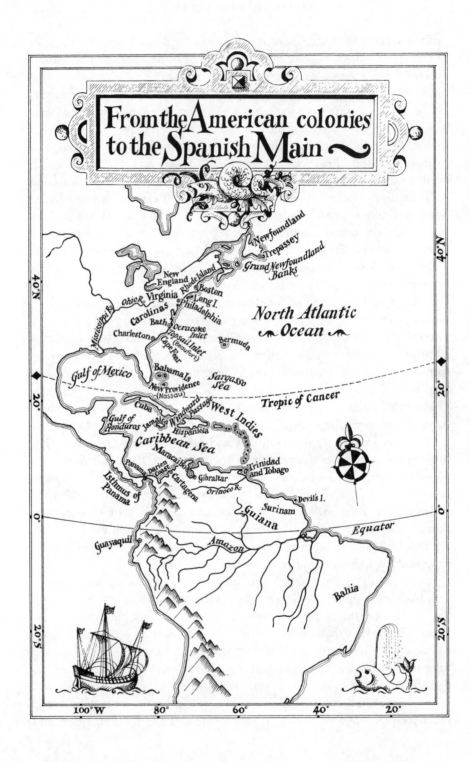

From the American colonies to the Spanish Main

Newfoundland
Trepassey
Grand Newfoundland Banks

New England
Rhode Island
Boston
Ohio R. Virginia Long I.
Carolinas Philadelphia
Mississippi R.
Bath
Ocracoke Inlet
Charleston Topsail Inlet (Beaufort)
Cape Fear

North Atlantic Ocean

Bermuda

Gulf of Mexico
Bahama Is.
New Providence (Nassau)
Sargasso Sea

Tropic of Cancer

Cuba
Windward Passage
West Indies
Gulf of Honduras Jamaica
Hispaniola
Caribbean Sea
Maracaibo
Panama Darien Coast
Cartagena Gibraltar Trinidad and Tobago
Isthmus of Panama
Orinoco R.

Devil's I.
Surinam
Guiana
Equator

Guayaquil
Amazon
Bahia

40°N

40°N

20°

20°

0°

0°

20°S

20°S

100°W   80°   60°   40°   20°

would promise not any further to annoy the Darien Indians, their allies, that then the buccaneers would desist from hostilities and go quietly about their business.' In answer to the question regarding the source of their commissions, Sawkins said with calculated bluff that as yet all his company were not come together, but that when they arrived he himself would visit him at Panama, bringing their commissions on the muzzles of their guns, at which time he should read them as plain as the flame of gunpowder could make them.

Learning also that the Bishop of Santa Marta was in the city, Sawkins sent him a present of two loaves of sugar, reminding him that he, the prelate, had been his prisoner five years before when he had captured that town. The bishop courteously acknowledged the gift and sent Sawkins a gold ring in return.

By now Sawkins had had intelligence of the approach of a rich galleon en route to Panama from Peru and wished to wait for its arrival; but, with supplies running low, the men became impatient for fresh provisions and persuaded him to sail south along the coast for the town of Pueblo Nuevo where they arrived on 22nd May.

The Spaniards, warned of their approach, had thrown up three strong breastworks at the entrance to the town, but Sawkins with characteristic daring leapt ashore ahead of his men, hair flying in the wind and cutlass and pistol in hand, to storm the defences, which he had barely reached when he fell before a withering Spanish fire.

And so died one of the last of the old buccaneer breed, the man whom nothing on earth could terrify, 'a man', as Ringrose was also to write, 'who was as valiant and courageous as any man could be, and the best loved of all our company'.

The succeeding fortunes of this expedition and those of subsequent Pacific ventures must be followed elsewhere. Sufficient to say here that the pioneer work of the leaders as explorers and their achievements in charting coasts, currents and prevailing winds, in describing the exotic flora and fauna they found and the customs of the strange tribes they encountered, were of lasting value.

Captain Howel Davis

Howel Davis was a member of the band of Welsh pirate captains who carved out for himself perhaps the most daring and ingenious career on record. He has the distinction of having stirred the admiration and regard of his biographers, as well as of a contemporary who knew and wrote of him at the height of his career.

Charles Johnson calls him a gamecock. Archibald Hurd describes him as a light-hearted daredevil with more than his share of Celtic dash and imagination who, given the chance, in happier circumstances, might have attained high rank among English admirals. Gosse recognizes his enterprise and success, and his preference for the use of strategy and cunning rather than force to gain his ends. A Captain William Snelgrave, who suffered severely at the hands of a pirate colleague of Davis and later published an account of his experiences, continually bemoaned the fact that he had not been taken by Davis – 'a most generous humane person'.

Davis was born at Milford, Pembrokeshire, and went to sea from an early age. He sailed out in 1718 on what was to be his last voyage from England as chief mate of a Bristol merchantman, the *Cadogan*, Captain Skinner master, bound for the Guinea Coast. Bristol at this time was, next to London, the richest, greatest and best port of trade in Great Britain, its sumptuous mansions and luxurious life-style financed, says a local annalist of the period, 'by the wealth made from the sufferings and groans of the slaves bought and sold by the Bristol merchant'.

The *Cadogan* had no sooner arrived at Sierra Leone, however, than it was captured by the pirate Edward England. This was a stroke of exceptional ill-fortune for Skinner who happened to be only too well-known to some members of England's crew since they had earlier served in his ship and, as the result of a quarrel, been handed over by him to a man-of-war and deprived of their wages. This was a device commonly employed by merchant captains for getting rid of troublesome seamen. Some captains, especially in wartime, would board a warship and – much to the anger of their crews – offer the services of some of the men, specifying by name those who would be most 'serviceable'! Tragically for Skinner, his ex-crewmen had managed to desert the warship, ending up on England's sloop. His capture now was sweet revenge for the disaffected seamen who seized him the moment he was brought aboard the pirate, and tortured him brutally before shooting him through the head.

With Skinner's death Edward England, who had only recently been forced into the role of pirate, appointed Davis captain of the *Cadogan*, and allowed him to sail her away under sealed orders which were not to be opened until he should come into a certain specified latitude. This was a surprisingly generous gesture, especially as the *Cadogan* was the first prize England had taken – a gesture which Davis, at any rate, attributed to the pirate's admiration of his courage in refusing to sign the articles.

Be that as it may, England's wishes were faithfully followed and at the place appointed, Davis opened the sealed document. This proved to be a deed of gift of the ship and contents to him and his men, with orders to proceed to Brazil, dispose of the *Cadogan*'s cargo and divide the proceeds fairly among the company. To Davis' surprise, however, most of the crew refused to follow England's directions. In a towering rage Davis told them they could go where they wished and be damned – which they proceeded to do by clapping him in irons, taking over the ship and sailing her to Barbados, to which island some of the cargo had been consigned. Davis was handed over to the authorities on arrival and thrown into prison, but was released three months later without being brought to trial as no actual charge of piracy could be laid against him.

But he was now a marked man. No one on the island was willing to employ him. In the circumstances he decided to make his way to New Providence where he felt his talents might be better recognized. The timing, however, was bad. Captain Woodes Rogers had arrived there shortly before, bringing with him the King's Pardon which most of the pirate fraternity had taken advantage of, many albeit with a wink. Still, things had changed. The pirate republic was no more. Gone were the wild days and wild doings of which Davis had heard so much in the waterside taverns.

So it was honest employment again for the Milford mate, for the present at least, and this was not long in coming as he soon managed to get a berth on one of two small sloops fitted out by Rogers for a trading voyage to the French and Spanish islands. One was the *Buck*, on which Davis sailed, the other the *Mumvil Trader*. Many of the hands were recently reformed pirates, of course, and Davis waited only for their arrival at Martinique when he and some like-minded crewmen rose at dead of night, clapped the master in irons, and seized the sloop. Davis then surprised the *Mumvil Trader* where he found a great many hands ripe for rebellion. He took everything out of her which might be of use and turned her over to the crew members who did not wish to join him.

As customary, a large bowl of punch was prepared and a council of war convened to choose a commander. The election fell unanimously on Howel Davis, whose short acceptance speech was a simple declaration of war against the whole world! A set of articles was then drawn up to which all present subscribed, most with a large and ill-formed 'X'.

The *Buck* being in need of cleaning, and, as the saying went, 'a light pair of heels was of great use both to take and to escape being taken', Davis sailed up the island chain to a small, secure inlet called Coxon's Hole at the east end of Cuba to careen. This done, he put to sea, cruising off the north side of Hispaniola where, with characteristic daring, he attacked and captured a twelve-gun French ship from which he took some much-needed provisions, in addition to other loot. Soon after, a sail was sighted away to windward which proved to be a heavily-armed Frenchman, mounting twenty-four guns and carrying a crew of sixty. This was a far more formidable challenge and Davis' crew had no stomach for it, but the crafty Welshman worked out a stratagem for taking the big ship, which he explained in detail to the crew, persuading them to trust him.

So, in the swift little *Buck* – scarcely bigger than a fishing smack – followed by the slower and heavier prize, Davis set off and soon overhauled the other Frenchman, which he hailed, ordering her to strike. Amazed at his impudence the French captain replied that if anyone was going to strike it would be he! But Davis had laid his plans well and, calling attention to his approaching consort, said he intended to keep them at play until she caught up, when they would be properly dealt with. By way of emphasis he spun the *Buck* round and gave them a broadside, which they returned.

In the meantime, as the prize drew near the prisoners on board, dressed in white shirts, were brought up on deck, as Davis had directed, to give a show of force, while a dirty bit of tarpaulin (the nearest thing on board to a Jolly Roger) was hoisted and a warning gun fired. Alarmed by this display of apparent force the French captain struck, as Davis had felt sure he would.

This was only the beginning of the wily Welshman's strategy. His succeeding moves are best described by Johnson:

Davis called out to the captain to come on board of him, with twenty of his hands; he did so, and they were all for the greater security clapt into irons, the captain excepted: then he sent four of his own men on board the first prize, and in order still to carry on the cheat, spoke aloud, that they should give his service to the captain, and desire him to send some hands on board the prize, to see what they had got; but at the same time gave them a written paper, with instructions what to do. Here he ordered them to nail up [spike] the guns in the little prize, to take out all the small arms and powder, and to go every man of them on board the second prize; when this was done, he ordered that more of the prisoners should be removed out of the great prize, into the little one, by which he secured himself from any attempt which might be feared from their numbers, for those on board of him were fast in irons, and those in the little prize had neither arms nor ammunition.

In this way the three ships sailed together for two days, but finding the larger prize to be a dull sailer, Davis gave her back to her captain with all his hands, having taken care to remove her ammunition and anything else which might be of use.

It is said that the French captain was so enraged at being so outwitted that he would have thrown himself overboard but for the quick action of some of his men in preventing him!

Devoted as he was to the plucky *Buck*, Davis let both prizes go and steering north took a Spanish sloop, then made for the Azores, but the pickings proving poor, steered south for the Cape Verde Islands, putting in at St Nicholas with English colours flying. Here he was well received by everyone, including the governor, did some profitable trading and spent a happy five weeks. When he finally sailed away, he was short of half a dozen hands who, charmed by the local ladies, had decided to settle there.

Davis then sailed to one of the other islands in the group, Bonavista, where he had a look at the harbour, but finding nothing of interest, went on to the island of Mayo. Here he was luckier. There were several ships in the road which he plundered at will, recruiting a number of eager hands and exchanging the *Buck* for a larger ship which he mounted with twenty-six guns and renamed the *King James*. He next put in at the neighbouring island of St Jago for water, posing as before for the benefit of the governor and other officials as a respectable trader, but for once his guile was seen through and the governor told him plainly he suspected he was a pirate. Davis was mightily affronted, of course, and protested his innocence, but made sure to return to his ship as fast as he decently could 'for fear of accidents'.

The crew was equally angry at the insult which had been offered their captain and it was decided to teach the Portuguese a lesson by sacking the place. This they succeeded in doing under cover of darkness, with the loss

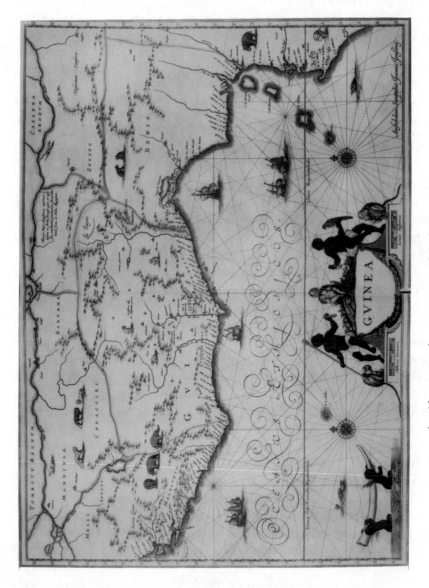

A mid seventeenth–century map of the Guinea Coast

of three of their number only. The fort was captured easily enough as the garrison had bolted for the governor's house where they barricaded themselves. Davis managed to throw some grenades inside, causing several casualties and doing much damage; he then dismounted the guns and sailed away as dawn broke before the townspeople could retaliate.

Honour had been satisfied and the Portuguese punished, but otherwise the effort had been profitless. The pirate company now numbered about seventy and a council of war was called to consider the next move. In view of Davis' experience of the African trade and wide knowledge of the coast, it was decided by a majority to make for the Gulf of Guinea where, encouraged no doubt by the success at St Jago, they would storm the Royal Africa Company's fort at the Gambia and relieve it of the money and goods usually stored there.

The fort was known, however, to be heavily garrisoned and some of the hands doubted that it could be successfully assaulted, but Davis was as reassuring as ever; he urged them to leave the management of affairs to him and he would make them masters of the place. The fact is, as Johnson says, 'They began now to conceive so high an opinion of his conduct, as well as courage, that they thought nothing impossible to him.' In this case, as in many others, their confidence was well placed.

As soon as the fort came in sight Davis sent all hands below, except those essential for the working of the ship, so as not to arouse any suspicions. He then ran close in under the fort and dropped anchor. Ordering out the boat, he, the ship's master and doctor, dressed discreetly as merchants, were rowed ashore by six crewmen wearing ordinary canvas jackets and tarred breeches so as to look the part of common sailors, having first been carefully instructed as to what to say, should they be questioned. The strategy worked. The trio were received by an armed guard of honour and conducted to the fort to meet the governor. Davis explained that they were Liverpool merchants, bound for the River Senegal to trade for ivory and gums, but who had narrowly escaped from two French men-of-war which had illegally come out after them.

However, they were prepared to make the best of a bad bargain and trade for slaves in exchange for iron and plate, a few textiles, some spirits and even a firearm or two. These were very desirable materials on the coast and the governor readily agreed to the deal, inquiring discreetly if they had any European liquor on board. Davis admitted that he had some, for their own modest use, but would be pleased to spare him a hamper, whereupon the governor invited them to stay and dine with him. Davis accepted with pleasure, but, pleading the need to return to his ship to see to her proper mooring and other matters, left the master and doctor with the governor, promising to return shortly with the hamper.

So far his plan had worked well. While in the fort he had taken careful note as to where the sentries were posted and the arms stored; he also saw that a great many small arms were kept in the governor's hall. Back on his ship he assured his men of success, urged them not to get drunk, and asked that as soon as the flag on the fort was struck they should immediately send a reinforcement of twenty hands ashore. Meanwhile, noticing a sloop that had come in since his arrival and anchored nearby, he sent a boat out to her, collared the captain and crew and clapped them in irons, just in case they might grow suspicious as to what was afoot and send a warning ashore.

He then selected his boat crew carefully, saw to it that each had two pairs of pistols concealed about his person (he himself would be similarly armed), instructed them to make their way to the guard room, get into friendly conversation with the soldiers there and, the moment he fired a pistol through the governor's window, to secure all the arms they could.

Davis arrived before dinner was ready and the governor proposed that they should pass the time over a bowl of punch, a suggestion that was greeted with delight. No sooner had the punch been prepared, however, than Davis, leaping up suddenly, drew a pistol, pressed it to the governor's breast and ordered him to surrender the fort or he was a dead man! The terrified governor promised to do as he was told. Meanwhile the master and doctor secured all the arms in the hall as Davis fired his signal shot through the window. Immediately his men sprang into action, covered the guards with their pistols, took out all the arms stored in the room, locked the startled soldiers in and mounted guard outside. Meanwhile the flag on the fort was struck and the reinforcements hurried ashore, as arranged. The coup was a complete success and pirate captain Howel Davis found himself master of one of the Royal Africa Company's principal stations, without the loss of a man on either side!

Davis next treated the soldiers of the garrison to a persuasive harangue, upon which most of them agreed to join his crew. Those who refused were put aboard the small sloop from which all sails and cables had first been taken out to prevent any chance of escape.

And now it was time to celebrate. A vast quantity of punch was consumed and numerous toasts proposed, especially to Captain Davis, which grew longer and more extravagant as the day wore on. All the while the station echoed to the roar of guns as the *King James* saluted the fort and the fort the *King James*.

The euphoria soon evaporated, however, when it was discovered that the bulk of the station's treasure had been shipped out shortly before Davis' arrival. All the same the pirates managed to collect some £2,000 sterling in bar gold and much valuable trade stores. They recompensed the master of the sloop they had temporarily commandeered with such items as they did not need, dismounted the guns of the fort and demolished the fortifications.

As they were preparing to sail out of port they spied a ship bearing down on them which Davis got ready to receive. This proved to be the French pirate Oliver la Bouche who had seen in the *King James* what he hoped would prove an attractive prize, but drawing closer he noted with misgiving the other's heavy armament and huge crew milling about on deck. Still, there was now no turning back, so firing a gun he hoisted the black flag and prepared to board. Davis, highly amused at this turn of events, returned the salute and floated out his own Jolly Roger, to the Frenchman's great relief.

There was much fraternizing aboard the ships and at la Bouche's suggestion it was agreed to sail down the coast together in the hope that he might secure a better vessel than the rather battered one he now commanded. Their first stop was at Sierra Leone where they found a tall ship at anchor which they felt exactly filled the bill. She seemed strangely unconcerned at the approach of the two vessels, however, and as Davis came alongside, she 'brought a spring upon her cable' – that is, came round in a different direction, gave Davis a broadside and hoisted the black flag. This Davis acknowledged with a gun to leeward and hoisted his own piratical colours. The ship belonged to a fellow freebooter named Thomas Cocklyn and Johnson tells us 'the satisfaction was great on all sides, at the junction of confederates and brethren in iniquity'. Two whole days were given up to drinking, spinning yarns and having a merry time together.

The three decided to join forces and attack the fort at Sierra Leone, which they did most efficiently, spending a week ashore, cleaning their ships and 'improving their acquaintance and friendship'. While there the *Bird* galley, Captain William Snelgrave, arrived at Sierra Leone river and anchored off the mouth. It was about seven in the evening, the date 1st April 1719, when the ship was surprised and seized by Cocklyn's crew. Snelgrave, an experienced seaman, intelligent and perceptive, was later to include an account of his ordeal in a book he wrote on the slave trade, published in 1734, which has been described as one of the most valuable single works in the whole vast pirate bibliography.

Snelgrave regarded himself as particularly unlucky to have been taken by Cocklyn and his men – 'a set of the basest and most cruel villains that ever were' – by whom he was barbarously treated. He had only good to say of Howel Davis: 'a generous man' who kept his crew of near 150 in good order. It was Davis who spoke up for him at the time of his capture, saying that 'he was ashamed to hear how I had been used by them; that they should remember their reasons for going a-pirating were to revenge themselves on base merchants and cruel commanders of ships; that he [Snelgrave] had not his fellow in London for generosity and goodness to poor sailors'. It was through Davis, in fact, that he gained his liberty. On 10th May he and his men finally embarked for England in one of the ships the pirates had left him before sailing away.

Calling a council of war the three freebooters agreed to sail down the coast in company, having conferred on Davis the grand title of Commodore of the little pirate squadron. But Davis' sure instinct told him it was an unworkable arrangement and must soon end. Already quarrels had broken out between them, especially when they had drunk too much. One evening, on board his ship, words almost came to blows and he decided to bring the alliance to an end.

'Hark ye, you Cocklyn and la Bouche,' he told them, 'I find by strengthening you, I have put a rod into your hands to whip my self, but I am still able to deal with you both; but since we met in love, let us part in love, for I find, that three of a trade can never agree.' At which the trio parted company and went their separate ways. They were never to meet again. La Bouche disappeared from history soon afterwards and Cocklyn ended his days on the gallows. As it happened, Davis' own ingenious career had almost run its course, although some daring and brilliant feats still lay ahead.

Holding his way down the coast, Davis soon met three merchant ships, two Scottish and one English, which he plundered in short order and sent on their way, but five days later, in the neighbourhood of Cape Three Points off what was to become known as the Gold Coast Colony, he fell in with a Dutch interloper with an armament of thirty guns and a crew of ninety, half of whom were English. A more prudent man would have avoided her, but not Howel Davis. He had barely drawn even than the Dutchman poured in a heavy broadside, killing nine pirates outright. Davis returned the fire and one of the hardest fights of his career began. The two ships fought from noon until nine the following morning when the disheartened Dutchman struck and called for quarter.

It had been a costly engagement, but Davis had got hold of a fine ship which he fitted up for his own use, and armed with thirty-two guns and twenty-seven swivels. He christened the ship *The Rover* and, in company with the *King James* which was now becoming leaky, sailed on to Annamabo. There he found three English ships, the *Hind*, the *Morrice* and the *Princess*, whose mate Bartholomew Roberts was soon to embark on a remarkable pirate career, trading for slaves, gold and ivory. Davis plundered all three, kept the *Hind* and the *Princess*, and made a present of the *Morrice* sloop to the Dutch captain, having first relieved her of 140 slaves, a quantity of gold dust and dry goods. He then traded shots with the fort which had had the temerity to fire on him, floated out his black flag and sailed off again down the coast with his flotilla.

Davis was now at the peak of his career with his most profitable capture only a day away. It was early the following morning that the masthead man spotted a sail. Lookouts on pirate ships were encouraged to keep their eyes skinned, for the articles usually provided that the man who first spied a sail that proved a prize earned, in addition to his share of the loot, the best pair of pistols on board. This was a prized perquisite as a good pair of pistols sometimes sold for as much as £30.

Davis immediately gave chase, but the ship, another Dutchman, swung towards the shore, intending to run aground rather than be captured. This Davis forestalled, caught up with her and fired a broadside, upon which she immediately struck. This was the Welshman's richest prize, and his last. On board was the governor of Accra returning to Holland with all his effects. In addition the ship carried a valuable cargo of merchandise and £15,000 sterling!

Davis gave the *Hind* and the *Princess* back to their respective masters, having recruited thirty-five of their men, including Bartholomew Roberts, for his own crew, restored the Dutch ship to her skipper, and, as the *King James* was now unseaworthy, took all her hands aboard his own vessel and abandoned her at anchor.

He now turned south towards the Portuguese colony of Princes Island (Príncipe), hoisting English colours as he approached. A small sloop was soon sent out by the governor to examine and make inquiries of the newcomer. Davis, with his customary craft, replied that he was a British man-of-war on the lookout for pirates who, he had been told, were on the coast. This sort of deception was possible at the time because the Royal Navy had not yet become a specialized service. No distinctive dress was worn, no navy lists were published. Many merchant vessels resembled warships both in construction and armament, and their crews were as ready to fire a broadside as loose a sail.

Satisfied with his answer, Davis was welcomed in the governor's name

c

and piloted into the harbour where he saluted the fort and anchored just under its guns. Hoisting out the pinnace, man-of-war fashion, he was rowed ashore where he was met by a guard of honour and conducted to the governor who received and entertained him warmly before he returned to his ship, promising to supply him with any provisions he might need.

So far all had gone well, but the arrival of a French ship on a supply mission proved too strong a temptation for Davis, who boarded and plundered her, justifying his action on the ground that he had discovered the ship had been trading with pirates and so he had seized the stolen goods in the King's name. The governor was satisfied with the explanation and, in fact, praised Davis for his percipience and zeal. But this was the first of three fatal mistakes which were to prove his undoing.

He discovered somehow that the governor and other officials kept their women friends safely secluded in a village inland and, with incredible indiscretion, Davis, with fourteen of his men, slipped secretly ashore and made their way towards this cosy harem, intending, as Johnson puts it, 'to supply their husbands' places with them'. But the ladies proved un-cooperative. With wild screams they fled into a neighbouring wood at the approach of Davis and company, who quickly sped back to their ship. The incident caused a considerable stir; however, as no one knew the identity of the would-be lovers, the fuss soon died down. But the affair was not at an end.

His ship cleaned and all things now ready for departure, Davis turned his fertile mind to the main business of his visit which was to plunder the island. His plan was simple and apparently foolproof. First he made the governor the handsome gift of fourteen slaves in return for his many kindnesses and invited him and his principal officials to a farewell banquet aboard his ship, which was readily accepted. The plan was that as soon as the governor and party arrived, they were to be seized, clapped in irons and held for a ransom of £40,000!

The night before, however, a black crew member of the plundered French ship who had discovered the plot and had learnt as well the identity of the visitors to the inland harem, managed to swim secretly ashore and reveal all to the governor, who determined to match cunning with cunning.

The following day Davis, accompanied by his chief officers, went ashore at the appointed time, as a mark of particular respect, to conduct the governor and party aboard. This suited the latter's purpose well. He met Davis and company most courteously and pressed them to come to his house for some refreshment before boarding the ship. They had no sooner started towards the residence, however, than they were caught in a deadly ambush from which only one crewman escaped alive. Davis himself was mortally wounded in the stomach, but managed to pull both pistols as he fell and shoot two of his attackers dead – 'like a game cock', says Johnson, 'giving a dying blow, that he might not fall unrevenged.'

Captain Bartholomew Roberts

'If a pirate is to be reckoned by the amount of damage he does and the number of ships he takes there can be no doubt that Captain Roberts should be placed at the very head of his profession,' writes Philip Gosse. No one questions this pre-eminence. Roberts *was* the most successful pirate of all, the most daring and most dreaded man at sea.

In only three years, between 1719 and 1722, he captured more than 400 ships, and his death, doing battle with a Royal Navy frigate, and the capture of his crew, symbolized the end of piracy's golden age.

Charles Johnson's account of Roberts is considerably longer than that of any other pirate, because, for one, as he says, he 'ravaged the seas longer than the rest'. The fact is, too, that Roberts' story is one of the best documented in pirate history, which is fortunate, for not only was he the most outstanding, but also virtually the last of the West Indian pirates, and his story is of historical as well as personal importance.

Roberts was born in 1682 near Haverfordwest, in Pembrokeshire, Wales, and went to sea as a boy, becoming in time a fine seaman and skilled navigator. We first hear of him in November 1719 as mate on the *Princess* galley, Captain Abraham Plumb, sailing from London to the Gold Coast to pick up a cargo of African slaves at Annamabo. Roberts would have been 37 years old then, a tall, handsome, dark-complexioned man.

The journey took three months and it was while the *Princess* was anchored off Annamabo taking in slaves for the West Indian market that she was captured by pirates in two well-armed ships, the *King James* and the *Royal Rover*, commanded by another Welshman Howel Davis, then at the peak of his own outstanding piratical career. Although Davis claimed never to have forced a man (a characteristic also attributed by some writers to Roberts), he took the latter aboard, perhaps to give him the chance to make up his mind. After careful thought Roberts decided to throw in his lot with the pirates (did he really have a choice?) and gave early proof of his courage and seamanship. He was later to admit that he took to the life, as much to be free of the tyranny of some masters of merchant ships, as for the

Captain Bartholomew Roberts

love of novelty and change to which seafaring had accustomed him. 'In an honest service', he once said, 'there is thin commons, low wages, and hard labour; in this, plenty and satiety, pleasure and ease, liberty and power; and who would not balance creditor on this side, when all the hazard that is run for it, at worst, is only a sour look or two at choking.'

The death of Howel Davis shortly afterwards during an unsuccessful action on the Portuguese slave-trading island, Princes Island (now Príncipe), fighting to the end 'like a game cock', raised the thorny question of his successor. This episode was to bring Roberts into contact with, and for a time command of some notorious practitioners in West Indian pirate history. These included Thomas Anstis who later deserted to forge an outstanding career for himself – he was eventually shot dead while asleep in his hammock by a disaffected crewman; Walter Kennedy, 'a bold daring fellow, but very wicked and profligate', whom Roberts appointed his lieutenant, but who also was to sneak off on his own in one of Roberts' prizes, only to end his days on Execution Dock; Valentine Ashplant who proved to be one of the leading lights of Roberts' company; and Henry Dennis, a Devonshire man, who remained faithful to Roberts. It was he who, over a bowl of rum punch, strongly pushed Roberts' candidature for commander, concluding his speech with: 'It is my advice that while we are sober, we pitch upon a man of courage, and skilled in navigation, one who by his counsel and bravery seems best able to defend this commonwealth . . . such a man I take Roberts to be.'

The speech was acclaimed by all, except by one David Sympson who had hoped to be elected himself, but seeing that he stood no chance, sulked off, muttering that he didn't care whom they chose as captain, so long as it wasn't a papist!

Roberts' acceptance speech, if not very graceful was at least frank: since he had dipped his hands in muddy water and must be a pirate, he told his assembled company, it was better being a commander than a common man.

One of Howel Davis' ships, the *King James*, becoming leaky and unseaworthy, had to be abandoned, so Roberts transferred his new command – between 100 and 120 men – to the *Rover*, mounting thirty-two cannon and twenty-seven swivels.

Roberts' first move – a popular one – was to avenge the death of Howel Davis. The fort commanding the harbour of Princes Island, built on a hill, was difficult to assault, but Roberts chose Kennedy to lead the storming party which, under cover of a heavy fire from the *Rover*, soon gained the heights. The garrison deserted to a man at the approach of Kennedy's wild bunch who poured in unopposed, rolled the guns down into the sea, set fire to the fort and marched back to their ship in high spirits. As a parting gesture Roberts fired two Portuguese ships to light him out of port that night.

Roberts stood away southwards, taking a Dutch Guineaman which he looted then gave back to her master, and later, an English ship *The Experiment* off Cape Lopez, recruiting the entire crew before burning her. He then stopped for water, provisions and a boot-topping job and, by popular vote, set sail for Brazil. Here, after initial disappointment, he stumbled upon a large Portuguese fleet of armed merchantmen in Bahia Harbour, about to sail for Lisbon under convoy of two warships, anchored off.

Although outnumbered forty to one, Roberts was not in the least bit daunted. Hiding most of his men below, he sailed boldly among the fleet, anchored alongside one of the ships, ordered her master aboard and calmly informed him that his life depended on his not resisting or raising an alarm. One look at the tall, daunting figure of 'Black Barty' and his evil-looking crew, emerging now with gleaming cutlasses and pistols at the ready, was sufficient to secure compliance.

At Roberts' request the master pointed out the richest merchantman in the fleet – a proud ship of 40 guns and 150 men. With incredible boldness Roberts sailed towards this ship hoping to take her by a ruse, but finding that suspicions had been aroused and that the crew were preparing for defence, he poured in a deadly broadside, killing several of her men, boarded and grappled her. The fleet, now fully alarmed, tried to attract the attention of the leisurely warships with gunfire signals and top-gallant sheets flying, but to little effect. Meanwhile Roberts, although hampered by his slow, deep-freighted prize, sailed calmly out of the assembled convoy and away!

This was perhaps the most daring capture in the history of West Indian piracy, and one of the most profitable. The Portuguese ship carried a rich cargo of sugar, hides and tobacco, as well as 40,000 moidores, worth some £50,000 sterling, together with jewellery including a cross set with diamonds destined for the King of Portugal.

Elated by their success, the pirates sailed up the Brazilian coast in search of a safe retreat where they might trade their loot and raise hell ashore, as only they could. Devil's Island, off the coast of what was to become French Guiana, proved to be the very place. Here not only the governor and local officials, but their wives also gave the pirates a royal welcome, and here they stayed for some weeks, enjoying what Johnson described as 'all the pleasures that luxury and wantonness could bestow'. So pleased was Roberts with the governor that he presented him with the diamond-set cross which had been meant for the King of Portugal.

From a small Rhode Island sloop which unwittingly entered the harbour and was seized by Roberts, it was learnt that her consort, a brigantine laden with provisions, was also on its way. With his own supplies now running low, Roberts and forty of his men sailed out in the captured sloop in pursuit as soon as the brigantine was sighted.

There is some confusion in the accounts of what happened next; however, according to Johnson, Roberts not only lost his quarry, but, beset by contrary winds and currents, became stranded far from base without sufficient food or water. In this extremity he sent the sloop's boat back to Devil's Island to order the ship to join them with supplies. When the boat eventually returned it was with the mortifying news that in Roberts' absence his lieutenant Kennedy had absconded with the *Rover* and the Portuguese prize.

Angered by this breach of faith (it was not to be the last) Roberts, perhaps naively, decided to draw up a set of binding articles, to be signed and sworn to by the whole company. The actual articles have not survived, but Johnson gives the substance of some of them, as related by the pirates themselves when they were eventually brought to trial.

They contained the familiar clauses respecting every man's right to the sharing of loot and to a vote in important affairs, the penalty for desertion, the need to keep their arms in fit condition for service, and so on; but some had less conventional features and are illustrative of the man's character. Article 3, for instance, forbade all gaming at cards or dice for money. Roberts is said to have been a total abstainer and drank tea only. If he had had his way there would have been no drinking on his ships, but this was, of course, impossible. Still, article 4, which he hoped would have acted as a check on the usual excessive drinking, required that all lights had to be extinguished by 8 pm, and that any crewman wishing to continue drinking thereafter must do so on deck. He allowed no boys or women aboard (a pointer to piratical sexual proclivities), the penalty for breaking this article being death. Roberts is seen as a strict Sabbatarian, because he allowed his musicians to have a rest on the seventh day. A unique article was the one that excluded all Irishmen from the company because Kennedy was Irish!

With Kennedy's defection Roberts was faced with the problems of restarting his career with only a small sloop, forty hands, no treasure or trade goods, and a shortage of provisions. Sailing for the West Indies he surprised a couple of merchantmen near the Windward Islands from which he fortunately got food, arms and ammunition. A few days later he took a brigantine belonging to Rhode Island, then sailing towards Barbados fell in with a Bristol ship on her voyage out laden with food supplies including oatmeal and beef, merchandise and ammunition, which he relieved her of, as well as of five crew members, before letting her go.

The ship immediately ran for Barbados with the news of his presence. As there were no men-of-war on the station at the time, a Bristol galley and a small sloop, then in port, were quickly armed and manned and sent in pursuit, falling in two days later with the pirates who, hoisting the Jolly Roger, fired a warning shot, expecting them to strike, but the galley with her twenty guns and crew of eighty answered with a galling broadside.

Further exchanges convinced Roberts of his mistake and he decided to run for it, crowding all the sail his sloop would bear, enduring a punishing fire from the galley meanwhile. He only got clear by heaving the guns and other heavy goods overboard to lighten ship.

It was a close call. His sloop had been badly damaged and thirty-five crewmen lost, but, characteristically, Roberts remained undismayed and was able to communicate his own confidence to his men. In contrast to most other pirate captains Roberts was an exceptionally intelligent as well as courageous man and, in spite of the usual difficulties, was able to command more respect from his crew than almost any of his colleagues.

Limping into a little-used bay on the lush, mountainous island of Dominica, Roberts watered and provisioned his ship, paying for what he got, and took on board a dozen Englishmen, possibly smugglers, set ashore there earlier by a French Martinique coastguard vessel. Sailing down the islands he hauled into a lagoon on Carriacou, in the Grenadines, where he cleaned with unaccustomed speed, there being, as his men later admitted, neither wine nor women to be had. This, as it turned out, was to prove their salvation, for two warships, sent after Roberts by the governor of Martinique, missed him by a few hours only, he having sailed overnight and the warships arriving the following morning.

It was now June 1720, and Roberts, moving with the seasons, sailed for Newfoundland, entering the harbour of Trepassey on the south coast with his black flag flying, drums beating loudly and trumpets blaring – an intimidating device he often used and which proved effective in this case, for the crews of the twenty-two vessels then in port instantly fled ashore, leaving the field open to the pirates.

For sheer wanton destruction this action is without parallel in pirate annals. Roberts plundered the port, burnt and sank all the ships he found, except a Bristol galley which he manned and mounted with sixteen guns.

Recruiting some willing new hands, he cruised on the Banks where he met and destroyed ten French ships, except one of twenty-six guns for which he swapped the Bristol galley, then sailed out on a very profitable trip taking ship after ship with impunity. These included the *Samuel* of London which carried a number of passengers and some £9,000 worth of the choicest goods. He forced four men out of her, including the sailing master, or 'sea artist' as the term was, named Harry Glasby who was to prove a thorn in his side. The pirates were particularly free and frank with the *Samuel*'s master, telling him, among other things, that should they ever be overpowered they would blow up their ship 'and all go merrily to hell together', which, as we shall see, they did intend to do. Roberts himself said often that he looked forward to nothing more than 'A short life, and a merry one'.

It is impractical to include here any but a select number of his hundreds of captures, or to follow him throughout his peregrinations which, as one biographer says, would be a liberal education in geography. The fact is that 'the great pirate Roberts', as he was now styled, plundered as he pleased, even in defended ports, to such an extent that the governor of Virginia, Alexander Spottswood, announced his intention of erecting coastal batteries as a precaution against a possible attack by Roberts!

Leaving Newfoundland Roberts made again for the West Indies and put in at St Kitts for supplies, but was rudely rebuffed. By way of response Roberts bombarded the town of Basseterre even while under fire from shore batteries, and burnt two ships in the road before dropping down to St Bartholomew where, in contrast, they were warmly welcomed and where they not only got all the supplies they needed, but all the women too, who vied with each other in attracting the good graces of such generous lovers who paid well for their favours.

Sated at length by this life of pleasure, the pirates voted to return to the coast of West Africa. On the way a French ship crossed their path with a valuable cargo which Roberts seized and took over, renaming her the *Royal Fortune*. Intending to make for Brava, the southernmost of the Cape Verde Islands, to clean ship, he appears to have missed his bearings, fell far to leeward and was obliged to go back with the north-east trades across the Atlantic. He decided to make for the coast of Surinam some 2,000 miles distant, but already short of food and water the crew of 124 men soon had their water ration reduced to one mouthful a day. Many died horribly and the survivors who eventually touched land at Surinam were little better than skeletons.

Once again the indomitable Roberts had pulled through and, rallying his remaining crew, he sailed towards Barbados, capturing two ships on the way well stocked with food and liquor. One of these was the *Greyhound*, bound for Philadelphia from St Kitts, whose mate joined the pirates and was later made captain of the *Ranger*, consort to the *Royal Fortune*. From there they made for the charming little island of Tobago for a short rest.

It was while in Tobago that Roberts learnt of the two warships sent to destroy him at Carriacou by the governor of Martinique. Consumed with anger he sailed up the island chain once more, vowing vengeance. It was now mid-February 1721 and, according to a news report, forwarded to the Council of Trade and Plantations by Governor Bennett of Bermuda, Roberts came up with a Dutch interloper at St Lucia with her yards and top-mast down. The pirates attempted to board, but she ran out her booms or fenders to prevent this, then began an obstinate resistance. The engagement lasted four hours and cost the lives of a number of pirates before the Dutchman struck. The unconfirmed report claims that the men found still alive on the Dutch ship were cruelly put to death: the usual penalty for resistance.

Refitting his prize, Roberts proceeded to put his subtle plan of revenge into effect. Knowing that it was the practice of the Dutch interlopers to hoist their jacks as they came in to trade their cargoes of slaves, he sailed slowly along the Martinique coast, making the appropriate signal, and was delighted to see sloop after sloop put out towards him. He was soon besieged by eager traders whom he welcomed aboard with his usual disarming courtesy. Then, to their dismay, he relieved each one of his cash, saying that he hoped they would always meet with such a 'Dutch trade'. He bundled them into one of the ships and burnt the others before sailing away. The same news report says the pirates barbarously abused the men they took, but this is unconfirmed: even Roberts' Christian name is wrongly spelt in the report.

Roberts never forgave the attempts by the governors of Barbados and Martinique to capture him, and went to the length of designing a personal flag with a depiction of himself, sword in hand, standing with each foot on a skull, under one of which were the letters A·B·H (for 'A Barbadian's Head'), and under the other A·M·H ('A Martinican's Head') – a pointed warning to the people of both islands of what to expect if they should fall into his hands. (See page 22.) He even had his personal cabin plate marked with the same device.

From Martinique Roberts threaded his way among the islands, seldom out of sight of land or of vessels to take, thence to the north side of Hispaniola to careen both his ships. While he was here two pirate sloops came in and the captains – Porter and Tuckerman – discovering Roberts' identity, paid him extravagant compliments, to the effect that 'they had put in there to learn his art and wisdom in the business of pirating . . . and hoped with the communication of his knowledge, they should also receive his charity, being in want of necessaries for such adventures'. Roberts was rather taken by the men, shared his powder, arms and other supplies and spent two or three merry nights in their company.

It was while here that Glasby and two of the crew attempted to desert the ship, but were captured and brought back. After a trial held in the ship's steerage, over a bowl of punch, all three were sentenced to death. Glasby was spared by the spirited intervention of one of the drunken judges, but the other two men were tied to the mast and shot dead.

This was the first sign of more serious trouble to come. In spite of the successful adventures the company had enjoyed, Roberts was now finding it increasingly difficult to hold his men together for, as Johnson says, 'being always mad and drunk, their behaviour produced infinite disorders', to which Roberts reacted by taking an increasingly tougher line. This ended in a serious quarrel between himself and a crewman named Jones who, although wounded by Roberts, managed to give the latter a thorough beating. Peace was restored by the quartermaster, and Jones was later flogged severely for his behaviour.

Roberts now quitted the West Indies and with his ship the *Royal Fortune* and a brigantine they had christened the *Good Fortune*, bent his course again for West Africa, but while still a considerable distance from the coast was deserted by Anstis in the brigantine, ably abetted by the disgruntled Jones, and some seventy hands. The loss of the brigantine was a sad one for she was an excellent sailer. However, Roberts continued on his course and arrived off the Senegal River towards the middle of 1721. Here the French had a monopoly of the trade in slaves, gums and ivory, maintaining two warships there to keep interlopers away. At sight of Roberts' sloop, which they mistook for a merchantman, the warships went out after him, but as the black flag rose, the Frenchmen's hearts sank and they surrendered without firing a shot. Roberts appropriated both vessels, one as his consort which he named the *Ranger*, the other as a store ship to clean by; then he went into Sierra Leone. Here it was that he first had word of the two Royal Navy ships, *Swallow* and *Weymouth*, of fifty guns each, the former commanded by Captain Chalenor Ogle, sent out to the coast to protect the African shipping from pirates. They had been in port about a month before and were not expected to return until Christmas.

It was now June 1721, and Roberts, his ships provisioned and his crew in high spirits from a good shore leave, sailed slowly down the coast plundering every ship they met and helping themselves to their cargoes. One of these, the *Onslow*, belonging to the Royal Africa Company, had a Church of England clergyman on board going out to one of the settlements, whom the pirates did their utmost to recruit, feeling that his presence would bring them the good fortune they deserved. His duties, they assured him, would be light: making punch and saying prayers. But the parson 'excused himself from accepting the honour they designed for him'. So in the end they released him, returning all his possessions (as well as those of some of his shipboard companions that he had particularly asked for) except three prayer books and a corkscrew.

Roberts exchanged his French ship for the *Onslow* and continued on his way, taking more prizes and frightening some French, English and Portuguese vessels he found off Whydah (now Ouidah), in the Bight of Benin, into paying him a ransom of eight pounds of gold dust each. It was here that he intercepted a letter to the Whydah agent of the Royal Africa Company from which he learnt that HMS *Swallow* was hard on his track. He explained the position to his men and it was agreed to weigh and sail for the island of Annabono (Annobón), but the wind hanging out their way brought him to Cape Lopez.

Fever meanwhile had broken out aboard the *Swallow* and Captain Ogle had to put in at Princes Island where he buried fifty of his men. Captain Herdman of the *Weymouth* had fared even worse. He had set out from England with a complement of 240 men and, at the end of the voyage, had 280 dead upon his books! Determined nevertheless to capture Roberts, Ogle sailed down the coast as soon as he could, checking all the likely hiding places, until 5th February 1722 when, arriving off the Cape, he spotted Roberts' ships.

The *Swallow* was forced to beat off a bit to avoid a sandbank at the entrance to the bay, a move which Roberts – unaware of *Swallow*'s identity – interpreted as a sign of alarm and he sent his consort the *Ranger* out to attack. Ogle, turning the misunderstanding to good advantage, kept away before the wind as though afraid, allowing the *Ranger* to approach only when they were both out of gunshot hearing of Roberts. The pirates then fired four chase guns, hoisted the dreaded black flag at the mizzen-peak, got their sprit-sail-yard under the bowsprit ready for boarding, and ordered the *Swallow* to come to. This the warship did, then suddenly hauling up her lower ports fired a staggering broadside into the *Ranger*.

The pirates fought with great spirit, losing ten men killed and many more wounded, including the commander, a Welshman named James Skrym who, with one leg shot away, continued to resist. An attempt to blow up the ship, in keeping with their avowed intent, was frustrated and the *Ranger* was eventually taken.

Ogle kept *Swallow* alongside the pirate only long enough to make her seaworthy, then sailed back to Cape Lopez where Roberts was still at anchor. He was at breakfast at the time enjoying a dish of salmagundy and took little notice at first of the approaching ship, but realizing eventually that she was the *Swallow*, he slipped his cable, crammed on all possible sail and ordered his men to arms, giving his orders with boldness and spirit. But even at that hour most of the crew were drunk – 'passively courageous' – and not fit for service.

Roberts made a fine and gallant figure on the deck, dressed in his rich damask waistcoat and breeches, a red feather in his cap, a heavy gold chain round his neck with a large diamond-set cross hanging from it, his sword in hand and two pairs of pistols hanging at the end of a silk sling flung over his shoulders.

His plan of action, a desperate one, was to sail out, black flag flying, close to the warship, receive her fire, return it, then make off as fast as he could. He might have succeeded, but at the crucial moment he lost the wind, perhaps through the ineptitude of his drunken crew. The *Swallow* came on a second time and Roberts was hit in the throat by grape shot. Even then with the remarkable strength for which he was noted, he heaved himself on to the tackles of a gun. The helmsman, seeing this, ran to his assistance, thinking him wounded only, but turning him round saw the ghastly death wound and blood-drenched damask waistcoat, at which, clasping his captain to him, he wept bitterly, praying that the next shot might be his. In keeping with his wish, Roberts' body was thrown overboard, fully dressed with all his arms and ornaments.

Without their dynamic leader the pirate crew soon lost heart and surrendered, most being later hanged by order of a Court of Vice-Admiralty held at Cape Corso (Cape Coast) Castle. On his return to England Ogle was knighted for his singular service in taking 'the great pirate Roberts'.

Captain George Lowther

George Lowther's story begins with the bare statement that he 'sailed out of the River of *Thames*' as second mate in one of the Royal Africa Company's ships the *Gambia Castle*, commander Charles Russell. This was in early 1721. In a short time he was to sail out of another well-known river in different circumstances, on a very different mission.

We do not know where Lowther lived, but it would almost certainly have been in London's East End, home of most of the city's seafaring population, probably in Rotherhithe or Wapping which face each other across the Thames. As he sailed out Lowther would have passed the notorious Execution Dock where so many pirates, mutineers and others had been 'seen off'. Farther down he would have sailed past Blackfriars stairs where the Newgate prisoners boarded the transports that took them to the American colonies as indentured servants. Then, into the 'Pool', the hub of the City's maritime activity, between London Bridge and the Tower. Finally, to Gravesend, last of the river towns – 'a right name as every body of Sailors knows' (in the words of one seaman) being a place where 'many never returne again'. Lowther was never to return again.

The *Gambia Castle* mounted sixteen guns and, in addition to her crew of thirty, carried a company of soldiers, under the command of Captain John Massey, who were to garrison a fort on one of the Africa Company's settlements on the River Gambia, captured and destroyed some time before by the Welsh pirate Howel Davis.

In May the slaver came safely to port and Captain Massey and his men landed. He was to hold command under the governor Colonel Witney who had arrived about the same time, but trouble started almost from the moment of arrival. 'The names of Governor and Captain sounded great', as Charles Johnson says, 'but when the gentlemen found that the power that generally goes with those titles was oversway'd and born down by the merchants and factors . . . they grew very impatient and dissatisfy'd', especially Massey who was outraged at the small allowance of provisions made to him and his men.

71

Massey, blunt soldier that he was, told them plainly that he had not come there to be a Guinea slave, that he had promised his men good treatment and provisions suitable for soldiers and if these were not forthcoming he would take appropriate measures for the care of his companions.

Meanwhile the governor, who had fallen seriously ill of a fever, was moved from the unhealthy, mosquito-infested settlement to the *Gambia Castle* where, as it happened, other discontents were brewing.

The captain had taken a dislike to Lowther who, fearful at his loss of favour, found means to ingratiate himself with the sailors to such an extent that on one occasion when Russell ordered Lowther to be flogged the men seized their handspikes and dared anyone to lay hands on him. The incident only served to widen the differences between captain and mate, while attaching Lowther more closely to the ship's company.

But the problem was more than one of a conflict of personalities. According to Lowther, the Royal Africa Company had neglected the seamen's health completely. They had arrived on the coast fit and well, but were soon in a 'miserable' state. There seems to have been difficulty also in securing a cargo of slaves and Lowther maintained that the attitude of the merchants was that the seamen could stay on the coast until they rotted.

This was the usual situation. The fact is, as Rediker points out, that seamen disliked the African trade more than any other for a number of reasons, chief among them being that of health. The African coast was deadly to English and American seamen who visited it. Malaria, yellow fever, scurvy and dysentery were common. The summer months were regarded as particularly dangerous. A seaman's doggerel summed up their attitude:

> Beware and take care
> Of the Bight of Benin;
> For one that comes out,
> There are forty go in.

The process of procuring a cargo of slaves often proved long, tedious and complicated, involving a stay of four months or more for slaver and crew. As desertion in the circumstances was virtually impossible, the merchants could take the attitude, as they did with the men of the *Gambia Castle*, that they could stay till they rotted.

Massey, meanwhile, whose discontent with the place and conditions grew daily, soon made common cause with Lowther and together they resolved 'to provide for themselves after another manner', which, as far as Massey at least was concerned, was to seize the ship and return in her to England. The soldiers were as eager as he to quit the country and, after spiking and dismounting the guns of the fort, they boarded the ship (Captain Russell being fortunately ashore at the time) and weighed anchor. Some vessels which lay near opened fire at the fugitive which was returned, but without damage on either side.

As the ship sailed out of the River Gambia, George Lowther knew there was now no turning back. As soon as they were well away at sea, he summoned the whole company and made them an impassioned speech. Knowing how Captain Massey felt, he began by saying that it was the greatest folly imaginable to think of returning to England, for what they had done could not be justified upon any pretence whatsoever, but would be looked upon, in the eyes of the law, as a capital offence, and that none of them was in a condition to withstand the attacks of such powerful adversaries as they would meet with at home – a caution which Massey was to ignore to his cost.

For his part, Lowther said, he was determined not to run such a risk, and therefore if his proposal was not agreed to, he asked only to be set ashore in some safe place. They had a good ship under them, a parcel of brave fellows in her, so there was no need for them either to starve or be made slaves; therefore, if they were all of his mind they should seek their fortunes upon the seas, as other adventurers had done before them.

His speech was greeted by loud cheers. We are told: 'They one and all came into the measures, knocked down the cabins, made the ship flush fore and aft, prepared black colours, and new named her, the *Delivery*.' A list of articles was then drawn up, signed and sworn to upon the Bible. George Lowther was now captain of a pirate crew.

His articles, which have come down to us, are interesting for a number of reasons, and they are set out here:

1. The Captain is to have two full shares; the Master is to have one share and a half; the Doctor, Mate, Gunner, and Boatswain, one share and a quarter.
2. He that shall be found guilty of taking up any unlawful weapon on board the privateer, or any prize, by us taken, so as to strike or abuse one another, in any regard, shall suffer what punishment the Captain and majority of the company shall think fit.
3. He that shall be found guilty of cowardice, in the time of emergency, shall suffer what punishment the Captain and majority shall think fit.
4. If any gold, jewels, silver, &c., be found on board of any prize or prizes to the value of a piece of eight, and the finder do not deliver it to the Quarter-Master, in the space of 24 hours [he] shall suffer what punishment the Captain and majority shall think fit.
5. He that is found guilty of gaming, or defrauding another to the value of a

shilling, shall suffer what punishment the Captain and majority of the company shall think fit.

6. He that shall have the misfortune to lose a limb, in time of engagement, shall have the sum of one hundred and fifty pounds sterling, and remain with the company as long as he shall think fit.
7. Good quarters to be given when called for.
8. He that sees a sail first, shall have the best pistol, or small-arm on board her.

These articles are based on typical privateering articles of the period – Lowther even calls his ship a privateer in article 2. Article 6 is of particular interest since the pension clause, compared with conditions in honest service, was particularly generous, while the provision of employment for disabled ex-crewmen was unique. Article 7, as we have seen, was almost always scrupulously observed by the majority of pirates, while the unstated punishment in articles 3, 4 and 5, although usually severe, was left to the decision of the ship's company as a whole, underlining the pirates' collective sense of transgression.

To return to Lowther and his crew: after about a week at sea they took their first prize a short distance from Barbados – a brigantine of Boston called the *Charles* – which they plundered thoroughly before letting her go. Steering a course for Hispaniola they overhauled a French sloop near the island's west end with a large cargo of wine and brandy. Captain Massey, posing as a merchant, went aboard the sloop and, inspecting the cargo with much apparent care, offered to purchase most of it. While discussing business, however, he contrived to whisper in the French captain's ear that he intended, in fact, to have the whole cargo . . . for nothing! Monsieur, we are told, quickly understood his meaning and agreed, although unwillingly, to the bargain.

Lowther and his men now boarded the sloop and relieved her of the wine and brandy, several pices of chintz and other valuable goods, as well as £70 currency, £5 of which Lowther generously returned to the French captain because of his civilities.

Matters, nevertheless, were not going well with the *Delivery*'s company. Massey had been a soldier from early youth and knew nothing about seafaring. Besides, he was a restless man of action who had to be doing something all the time. Irked by the slow pace of life at sea, he asked Lowther to let him have thirty men with whom he would attack one of the French settlements, promising to bring aboard 'the Devil and all of plunder'!

The level-headed Lowther did his utmost to dissuade Massey from so rash an undertaking, pointing out to him the danger to which the whole company would be exposed if the venture failed, but Massey was adamant, so Lowther was forced to put the matter to the vote. Although Massey had his supporters, the majority of the company opposed the scheme. This only served to inflame the fractious officer and a quarrel broke out which soon divided the ship's company between those who sided with the would-be *Land-pirate* and those with the *Searover*. The disagreement had reached a dangerous point when the ringing cry of 'A sail! A sail!' from the masthead man sent the whole company rushing to action stations, with all else forgotten for the present.

The sail proved to be a small ship from Jamaica bound for England, which they caught up with in a few hours, taking out of her what they thought fit, as well as a hand or two, before letting her go on her way. But the problem with Massey remained.

The following day they captured a small sloop which they detained. Massey now openly declared his intention to leave the company and Lowther agreed that he, and all hands who had a mind to go with him, should have the sloop and be gone. Ten of the *Delivery*'s men joined Massey, and Lowther doubtless sighed with relief as they boarded the small sloop and bore away for Jamaica.

The rest of Captain Massey's story may be briefly told. On arrival in Jamaica he went straight to the governor, Sir Nicholas Lawes, to whom he surrendered himself and his ship and frankly confessed to everything that had happened since his arrival in Africa. The governor received him well, gave him his liberty and, at Massey's earnest request, allowed him aboard the *Happy* sloop, commanded by Captain Lawes, to cruise off Hispaniola in search of Lowther, but, as it happened, without success.

Back in Jamaica he managed to secure a certificate from Sir Nicholas and the funds necessary for a return passage to England. Here the simple, plain-spoken officer admitted to all that had taken place since he had sailed out of Africa, throwing himself on the clemency of the authorities, asking only that, if they were determined to prosecute him, he might not be hanged like a dog, but be shot, and so 'die like a soldier, as he had been bred from his childhood'. But, as Lowther had predicted, even this was not to be: he was brought to trial before a Court of Admiralty, found guilty and hanged at Execution Dock.

Lowther, meanwhile, after cruising off Hispaniola, played to windward and near Puerto Rico chased two sail, one a small Bristol ship, the other a Spanish pirate. He rifled both vessels and then burnt them, pressing the English crew into service and sending the Spaniards off in their launch, putting at least one foreign competitor out of business.

By now his ship, renamed the *Happy Delivery*, was in sore need of cleaning, and his crew of some recreation ashore. A small sloop belonging to St Kitts which crossed his path was quickly taken, manned and carried along to a nearby island, the name of which is not recorded but where Lowther and his men were to find the ideal conditions for careening, as well as indulging in what the moralizing Johnson calls 'unheardof debaucheries' – drinking, whoring, rioting, swearing – 'in which', he says, 'there seemed to be a kind of emulation among them, resembling rather devils than men, striving who should outdo one another in new invented oaths and execrations'.

They stayed on the island until Christmas when they took to sea again and sailed towards the Bay of Honduras, the popular pirate rendezvous, stopping en route at Grand Cayman for water. Here they found a small vessel, anchored close to a whitesand beach, with only thirteen hands, commanded by one Edward Low, then at the start of a noted piratical career of his own. At Lowther's suggestion Low scuttled his little boat and transferred his small company to the *Happy Delivery* where he was appointed lieutenant.

They came into the Bay in early January and promptly fell upon a Boston ship of 200 tons, the *Greyhound*, commanded by Benjamin Edwards. Hoisting the Jolly Roger Lowther fired a warning shot for the *Greyhound* to bring to, but getting no response he gave her a broadside which was returned and a brisk engagement followed. Captain Edwards fought bravely, but finding the pirates too strong for him, struck his ensign. Over the vessel's side poured the angry pirates, slashing, beating and maltreating the crew – the penalty always for resistance – then rifling the ship they set her on fire.

Cruising leisurely about the Bay they met and took a number of vessels, mostly American, but including a Jamaican sloop which they kept for their own use, as well as a Rhode Island ship of 100 tons, mounting eight carriage and ten swivel guns, to which Admiral Lowther (as he was now styled) transferred his lieutenant Edward Low.

Sailing out of the Bay Lowther's little fleet steered for the Gulf of Amatique on the Guatemalan coast, making for what they hoped was a safe, secluded cove in which to careen, but this time their choice of a careenage proved unfortunate. They had no sooner got the spoil and supplies ashore than they were attacked by a large body of fierce and well-armed Indians and forced to retreat to the ships, abandoning their possessions and the *Happy Delivery* which the attackers destroyed by fire – an unlucky augury, as events were to show.

The loss of their hard-won loot was a bitter enough blow, but the loss of their supplies was to bring the small company close to disintegration. Crammed aboard the largest ship of the fleet, the *Revenge*, smarting from the unexpected turn of events, short of food and water, the company, says Johnson, was thrown into 'a confounded ill humour, insomuch that they were every now and then going together by the ears, laying the blame of their ill conduct sometimes upon one, then upon another'.

In early May 1722 they reached the West Indies where, fortunately, they took a brigantine well stocked with the provisions they needed. Tempers rapidly improved, as did business for, standing northwards towards the American coast, they took yet another brigantine, out of St Kitts, which helped Lowther solve the problem of what to do with Captain Low who, by now, had become unruly and difficult to handle, aspiring clearly for the post of commander. So, according to the vote, they parted company, Low going off aboard the brigantine with forty-four hands to seek his fortune, and Lowther, with the same number of men, aboard the sloop, proceeding on his own way. Low, who was almost certainly insane, is remembered chiefly for his appalling cruelty.

Sailing up the coast of Maine Lowther took three or four fishing vessels and a New England ship out of Barbados whose cargo, a varied one, included fourteen hogsheads of rum, six barrels of sugar, a considerable quantity of pepper, money, plate and six black slaves.

Turning southwards again Lowther dropped slowly down the American eastern seaboard to South Carolina where he spied the ship *Amy* just come out on her voyage to England. He promptly hoisted the black flag and fired a warning shot across her bows, but Captain Gwatkins, master of *Amy*, was not impressed and answered with a broadside. There was something about the vessel's posture that warned Lowther, instinctively, of possible danger and he decided to make off, but the plucky Gwatkins, getting his ship between the pirate and the shore, stood after him, intending to board. To prevent this Lowther was forced to run his sloop aground and make for the shore with his men and weapons. But Captain Gwatkins was not finished with the pirate. He quickly lowered a boat and set off towards the stranded sloop intending to set her on fire, but was killed by a well-aimed shot from the shore before he reached the ship. The *Amy*'s mate, not being inclined to pursue the fight any further, took charge of the ship and sailed away.

This was Lowther's first serious setback, one from which he was never fully to recover. With the *Amy*'s departure he got his sloop afloat again, but she had been badly damaged in the brief engagement. Besides, a great many of his old hands had been killed, especially among the gun crews, while a number of others were badly wounded. He managed to sail his shattered ship into an inlet on the North Carolina coast where he was to remain a long time before he could put to sea again.

Here he and his crew laid up all the dismal winter, shifting as best they could. In the daytime, divided into small parties, they hunted the scrawny black cattle and meagre hogs in the woods for food, huddling together by night in rude huts and in tents made from the sloop's sails. When the weather turned too cold they climbed back aboard their ship for shelter.

With the coming of spring they managed to get to sea and steering a course for Newfoundland took a schooner on the Banks amply stocked with the provisions they so desperately needed. Pressing three members of the crew, they let the schooner go. Several other vessels in the neighbourhood fell into Lowther's clutches before he steered once more for the warm, sunlit Caribbean where he cruised with moderate success, but plagued, as often before, by a shortage of provisions.

By now the sloop was badly in need of cleaning and Lowther pitched on Blanquilla, a small island some ninety miles north of Cumaná, Venezuela, for the purpose. Blanquilla was a delightful island, low and even, healthy and dry, about six miles in circumference, with large groves of lignum vitae trees and shrubby bushes. The iguana bred in numbers on the island, as did the succulent sea turtle, the meat of both being much prized by the pirates who used the place for careening. The land went sheer down to deep water all round the coast, except at the north-west end where there was a small, whitesand cove. Here Lowther unrigged his sloop, sent guns, sails and rigging ashore and put his vessel upon the careen. Blanquilla island was to be his last landfall.

The careen was almost complete when the *Eagle* sloop of Barbados, belonging to the South Sea Company and commanded by Walter Moore, sailing close to the island on its way to Cumaná, spotted Lowther's ship and grasped the opportunity to attack her. The pirates quickly cut their cable and hauled the ship's stern ashore, forcing the *Eagle* to come to anchor athwart their bow where she engaged them. Unprepared as they were, however, resistance was fruitless and, calling for quarter, the pirate struck, but Moore was merciless. Lowther and twelve of his men managed to escape through a cabin window and make for the island's wooded interior.

After getting the sloop off and securing her, Moore and some of his hands went in search of the pirates, but after nearly a week in the woods they only succeeded in capturing five. Four more were caught later by a search party sent out by the Spanish governor of Cumaná, but Lowther was never taken.

Secure amid the deep shadows of the splendid groves, surrounded always by the sound of the surf pounding on the rockbound coast and, when he ventured down to the ill-fated cove, by the soft hiss of the calm water on the white sands, George Lowther's thoughts must have turned often to that last voyage down the Thames as second mate of the slaver *Gambia Castle* and of the strange sequence of events which were to bring him to this last anchorage.

He must have sat at times, his back against the cool, smooth trunk of a lignum vitae, his loaded pistol always within reach, and watched the tiny, blue-mauve blossoms drifting down in the soft sea breeze, for it was here, long after, that he was found by some sloop's men – dead, with his pistol 'burst by his side'.

Captain Charles Vane

The glamour surrounding the story of 'Calico' Jack Rackham and his unique female crew members tends to overshadow that of his original leader Charles Vane, from whom he learnt much; but Vane was a notable pirate captain in his own right, brave, resourceful, mercurial, and, in some respects, more successful than the flamboyant Rackham.

Most accounts of his career begin with a typical Vane gesture. Captain Woodes Rogers, the newly appointed governor of the Bahamas, had arrived with his small fleet off the bar of New Providence harbour on the evening of 26th July 1718. He was told there were over a thousand pirates in the port waiting for the long expected King's Pardon which he had brought with him. The exception was Charles Vane.

Vane had turned up in New Providence some time earlier, sword in hand and lording it over the inhabitants. We are told he reigned there for three weeks and on being informed that a governor was on his way from England, swore that while he was in port he would suffer no other governor than himself! He was in fact preparing for a cruise when Woodes Rogers arrived and blockaded the harbour. Vane immediately decided to open negotiations with the governor on his own account, sending him a letter stating that he would accept the Pardon only if he could dispose of his spoil in any way he wished, but not receiving an answer he determined to make for the open sea.

That night a fire and explosion near the town was mistaken by Rogers and company for a pirate celebration at the forthcoming amnesty, but proved to be Vane firing a French prize ship he could no longer use. Borrowing a sloop from his friend Yeates that was light enough to get out of the harbour by the east passage which had been left open, he loaded her with his loot and such provisions as he needed, then pressing the island's best carpenter and pilot into service, he and forty of his old hands slipped their cable at daybreak and sailed out, hoisting the black flag and firing a defiant shot in the governor's direction as they went by!

Woodes Rogers immediately dispatched two well-armed ships in pursuit, but Vane, easing out his mainsheet and setting his flying-jib, easily outdistanced them. He later sent the governor a message promising to pay him a visit and burn his guardship for his impudence in chasing him instead of answering his letter; but, in fact, he was never to return to the Bahamas, although he continued to be of great concern to Woodes Rogers because of his repeated threats to come back and drive him out.

There appear to be only two items of information about Vane pre-dating this episode. One, from Charles Johnson, concerns his role in helping to relieve the Spaniards of a rich hoard of silver which they had salvaged from galleons wrecked by a hurricane in the Gulf of Florida in 1715, which is very much in character. The other is contained in depositions forwarded in May 1718 by the governor of Bermuda to the Council of Trade and Plantations alleging brutal treatment of the crews of certain Bermuda vessels captured by Vane on their way to the Turks Islands to load salt.

One deponent, Nathaniel Catling, mariner on the Bermuda sloop *Diamond*, taken on 17th May 1718, claimed that after beating the whole crew, Vane's men hanged him by the neck until they thought he was dead, but seeing that he was reviving, a pirate slashed him with a cutlass over the collarbone, and had to be restrained by his fellows.

The other, Edward North, commander of the *Edward and Mary* sloop, deposed that he was captured by Vane on 14th April 1718 and maltreated; that Vane's men bound one of his company, hand and foot, and tied him on to the bowsprit, putting lighted matches near his eyes and pushing the muzzle of a pistol into his mouth, 'to oblige him to confess what money was on board'.

These stories are not in character with the accounts of Vane's other activities that have come down to us. Of course, if a pirate suspected that valuables were being concealed from him – as seems to have been the case with the *Edward and Mary* – he was not too tender-hearted about the methods used to force a confession. The buccaneers were even less so. Good treatment was usually the reward for handing over the loot. Besides, he had what he at least regarded as good reason to dislike Bermudans, because they had detained one Thomas Brown who should have sailed with him, 'upon suspicion of piracy'.

However, after escaping Woodes Rogers' wrath, Vane's luck held, as usual, and two days out he captured a Barbados sloop in which he placed Yeates with twenty-five hands, taking another merchantman two days later, with a cargo of pieces-of-eight, which he also added to his small fleet. He then made for a secluded islet where he careened, shared out the loot and, says Johnson, 'spent some time in a riotous manner of living, as is the custom of pirates'.

The carouse over, Vane beat up for the Windward Islands where he took a Spanish ship on its way to Havana, looted and burnt it, stowing the crew in a small boat so that they might find their way back to Puerto Rico. By now provisions and other stores were running low – always a problem with pirates who, of course, had no home base. However, steering between St Kitts and Anguilla Vane fell in with a brigantine and a sloop with the very cargoes he needed.

He now sailed towards the North American colonies where, in August, he operated off the Carolina coast, much to the distress of the Charleston community who had endured unwelcome visits shortly before from Stede Bonnet and the dreaded Blackbeard. Ranging back and forth Vane took and looted ship after ship, including one out of Barbados, another from Antigua, a third from the Dutch island of Curaçao and a large brigantine from the Gulf of Guinea, in West Africa, with ninety slaves on board, bound for Charleston under the command of a Captain Thompson. Vane moved the slaves to Yeates' sloop which, by a quirk of fate, was to prove the means of Thompson's eventually recovering his human cargo.

As it happened, by now relations between Vane and Yeates had become strained. Vane, Johnson tells us, always treated his consort with scant respect, assuming a superiority over him and his small crew and treating the other's vessel as a mere tender to his own. Yeates had put up with this for a long time, but the breaking point came with the arbitrary transfer of so many slaves to his ship with so few hands to care for them.

A couple of days later, as the pirate fleet lay at anchor some thirty miles south of Charleston, in the vicinity of the North Edisto River, Yeates decided that the time had come to part company with his chief. As evening came on he slipped his cable, hoisted sail and stood into the shore. Vane, who was 'highly provoked' by Yeates' defection, immediately gave chase. His brigantine was the faster sailer and would have overhauled the fugitive had the run been longer, but as he came within gunshot Yeates made it over the bar and, firing a broadside at his old friend, took his leave.

Yeates and his comrades later received certificates of pardon from Governor Robert Johnson of Charleston, and Captain Thompson recovered the slaves Vane had taken from him.

During this time Vane was 'wrathfully cruising' outside the bar of the North Edisto River hoping that Yeates would appear, keeping his hand in the while, so to speak, by taking and plundering two more vessels on their way to Charleston from England. Meanwhile Governor Johnson had fitted out two well-armed sloops under the command of the Receiver-General Colonel William Rhett, to go in search of Stede Bonnet who was believed to be lying up in Cape Fear River. Rhett was about to sail when he learnt of Vane's presence and decided to go after him instead. The reports he got said Vane was sailing southwards to careen, but this story the wily pirate had put out to throw Rhett off the scent when, in fact, he had sailed north past Cape Fear and put in at Ocracoke Inlet. This was a lucky chance for here he ran into his renowned colleague Edward 'Blackbeard' Teach whom he saluted with his great guns loaded with shot (as was the custom when pirates met) fired wide or up into the air. Blackbeard answered the salute in like manner and 'mutual civilities passed for some days'.

After the celebration Vane took his leave and continued northwards. Towards the end of October he captured a small brigantine and a sloop off Long Island, thence he and company cruised between Cape Maisí at the eastern tip of Cuba and western Hispaniola without seeing or speaking with any vessel, until the end of November when they fell in with the French man-of-war which, as mentioned in the account of Rackham, Vane declined to attack: a decision that, although perhaps prudent, was to lead to his being turned out of the company and Rackham, the quartermaster, elected in his place.

Vane had argued that the man-of-war was too strong for them to cope with.

Rackham agreed that she had more guns and greater weight of metal, but felt that they might be able to board her 'then the best boys would carry the day'.

Vane, however, thought the enterprise too rash and desperate. The man-of-war appeared to be twice their force and their brigantine might be sunk before they could get close enough to board.

Vane had his supporters, including Robert Deal the mate and fifteen others, but the vote went against him. Rackham, by now presumably Yeates' successor, had 'a kind of check upon the captain', says Johnson, and carried the day. Even so, Vane's reputation and forceful personality ensured him respectful treatment. He and the crewmen who had sided with him were allowed to have a small sloop, captured some time before, stocked with a sufficient store of provisions and ammunition 'that they might be in a condition to provide for themselves, by their own honest endeavours', which Vane lost no time in doing, as Captain Rackham sailed away to fulfil his own destiny.

Vane and his small company now headed for the Bay of Honduras, the pirates' southern rendezvous, putting their small craft in as good condition as they could along the way. Then, cruising for two or three days off Jamaica's north coast, they captured a sloop and two piraguas, the crews of which readily joined the pirate company. Discarding the dugouts, Vane kept the sloop, to which he transferred Deal as captain.

It was now 16th December and Vane fell in with an armed vessel – the *Pearl* of Jamaica, Captain Charles Rowling – which promptly got under way at sight of Vane. Seeing, however, that the sloops stood towards him, showing no colours, Rowling gave them a gun or two, at which Vane broke out the fearsome black flag and responded with heavy gunfire. The *Pearl* struck, was captured and carried away to the small island of Bonacca (one of the Bay Islands, now called Guanaja) to careen, meeting yet another luckless Jamaica ship on the way, which they made prize of.

Taking his ease ashore while his ships were scraped clean, presiding over the division of the loot, drinking and dallying, doubtless, with the local doxies, feasting on turtle meat, fresh fruit and provisions, the pirate chief would have had good reason to be satisfied with the way things had gone. He had made a fortune and a name for himself, bid defiance to a British colonial governor, spurned His Majesty's Pardon and survived an ignominious expulsion from his former command to become leader once more of a freebooter fleet.

Here he spent Christmas, laying up in safe obscurity, until February of the following year, unaware of what was happening in the Caribbean, and perhaps not caring; not knowing that his fellow rover Blackbeard had died, drinking and shouting defiance to the end; that James Fife, who had accepted the amnesty at New Providence he had spurned, had been killed by his own men; that John Martel's crew were destroyed and he marooned; that Nicholas Brown, 'the Grand Pirate', and his friend Christopher Winter had surrendered to the Spaniards at Cuba; and not dreaming that the cruise he himself was about to embark upon was to be his last.

Vane sailed in February, but was only a short time out when a violent freak storm overtook him. For two days his ship ran helplessly before the wind, being driven at length upon a small uninhabited island in the Bay of Honduras where she foundered with most of the crew. Vane survived, dragging himself ashore, half-drowned, with nothing but the ragged clothes he wore.

Here he languished for some weeks, depending for food on the charity of a few poor fishermen who visited the island from the Main in small craft in search of turtles. Then his luck seemed to change with the arrival of a ship from Jamaica which had put in for water, commanded by a Captain Holford, an ex-buccaneer and an old friend of his. Vane promptly asked Holford for a berth on his ship, but this the smart old Brother of the Coast firmly refused.

'Charles,' he said (according to Captain Johnson), 'Charles, I shan't trust you aboard my ship, unless I carry you a prisoner; for I shall have you caballing with my men, knock me on the head, and run away with my ship a-pirating.'

Vane made all the protestations of honour in the world, but Holford was not to be moved: 'I am now going down the Bay', says he, 'and shall return hither, in about a month; and if I find you upon the island when I come back, I'll carry you to Jamaica, and hang you.'

'Which way can I get away?' answers Vane.

'Aren't there not fishermen's dories upon the beach? Can't you take one of them?' replies Holford.

'What,' says Vane, suitably outraged. 'Would you have me steal a dory then?'

'Do you make it a matter of conscience', asks an exasperated Holford, 'to steal a dory, when you have been a common robber and pirate, stealing ships and cargoes, and plundering all mankind that fell in your way? Stay there, and be d———n'd, if you are so squeamish,' with which the reformed buccaneer left him and sailed away.

Even then fortune still seemed to favour Vane, for a few days later another vessel bound for Jamaica put in to the island for water. Neither the captain nor any of his crew knew Vane who, giving an assumed name and posing as a poor, hardworking castaway, was shipped for the voyage. But, in fact, Vane's luck had at last run out.

It happened that Captain Holford, returning from the Bay, fell in with the ship that had rescued Vane, and the captains knowing each other well, Holford was invited aboard to dine. As he passed along his way to the great cabin he happened to look down the hold where he spied Vane hard at work. He immediately called his host – and here Johnson again takes up the narrative, complete with dialogue:

'Do you know who you have got aboard here?' asks Holford.

'Why I have shipped a man who was cast away in a trading sloop, he seems to be a brisk hand,' answers the other.

'I tell you', says Holford, 'it is Vane, the notorious pirate.'

'If it be him, I won't keep him.'

'Why then,' says Holford, 'I'll send and take him aboard, and surrender him at Jamaica.'

This was agreed to and Vane was put in irons and transferred to Holford's custody who on arrival at Jamaica 'delivered his old acquaintance into the hands of justice; at which place he was tried, convicted, and executed', concludes Johnson.

Although credulously repeated by writer after writer, there is reason to question how much of this part of Vane's story is fact and how much fiction. The fictitious dialogue apart, did Holford really bring Vane in? If so, why did the Jamaica House of Assembly, at its meeting on 24th March 1720, pass two resolutions, one that in its opinion Captain William Magarity had done 'a considerable service to the country in taking Charles Vane, a notorious pirate', the other approving the payment to Magarity of a £100 reward 'for such service'?

Still, it was all one, in the end. Vane was tried at a Court of Vice-Admiralty held in Spanish Town on 22nd March 1720, presided over by the redoubtable Governor Lawes. Some of his sins – sufficient to secure a conviction – are recounted in the Articles exhibited at the trial and supported by the witnesses called. He was found guilty of piracy, condemned and hanged one week later on infamous Gallows Point, and, like his old mate Jack Rackham, had the distinction of being stuffed into a suit of iron and gibbeted on Gun Cay, off Port Royal.

It is perhaps fitting that, when the time came, the notorious Captain Charles Vane 'showed not the least remorse for the crimes of his past life'.

Captain Teach or 'Blackbeard'

Have you heard of Teach the Rover
And his knavery on the Main,
How of gold he was a lover
How he loved all ill-got gain?

The story of Captain Edward Teach – perhaps the most famous pirate who ever lived – is full of contradictions. These begin with his very name and origin. Charles Johnson called him Thatch in the first edition of his *History* and later Teach. Other forms of the name (some appearing in official records) are Tach, Tache, Tatch, Teatch and Teague, with the alternatives Drumond and Drummond!

Johnson says he was a Bristol man; elsewhere he is described as a native of the Carolinas, while a contemporary, Charles Leslie, in his *New History of Jamaica* (1740), says he was born in Jamaica of very creditable parents, that his mother was living in the capital Spanish Town in his (Leslie's) day, and that his brother was captain of the train of artillery. However, a search of the relevant Jamaican parish registers has failed to produce a record of his birth.

Leslie states that Teach was of a most bloody disposition and 'cruel to brutality', while Johnson calls him a hardened villain who 'would not stick at perpetrating the most abominable wickedness imaginable'. He does admit he was a good sailor, bold and daring to the last degree.

On the other hand, Patrick Pringle, who used official records extensively for his account of Teach, says he was not guilty of a single atrocity, treated his prisoners humanely, rarely had to fight, was avoided by the Royal Navy and protected by the governor of North Carolina!

The truth might be, as another biographer puts it, that no other pirate was more notorious (if for the wrong reasons) in his day, or afterwards more fearsome in anecdote and legend. For this, more than anything else perhaps, Teach had to thank his remarkable black beard, the source of his nickname – 'that large quantity of hair which, like a frightful meteor, covered his whole face and frightened America more than any comet that has appeared there a long time', in Johnson's words. Teach allowed his famous beard to grow to an extravagant length, plaited it into a hundred tails twisted with ribbons and turned up about his ears. When going into action he stuck slow-burning hempen cords soaked in saltpetre into the plaits and under his hat which, blazing on each side of his face, his naturally fierce and bloodshot eyes glaring through the encircling smoke, made him altogether such a figure, declares Johnson, 'that imagination cannot form an idea of a Fury from Hell to look more frightful'.

Johnson says Teach sailed out of Jamaica in privateers during the War of the Spanish Succession. Although the war was fought in Europe, defensive operations in the Caribbean required the services of a number of distinguished naval officers, as well as the support of privateers on both sides. By 1707 Britain had some twenty-four warships in West Indian waters, but they were far from sufficient and English settlements and commerce suffered severely from the activities of French and Spanish privateers.

Teach distinguished himself during this time for his uncommon boldness and personal courage, but did not manage to secure a position of command. With the end of the war in 1713 he and hundreds of other privateersmen would have been thrown out of work, with little to show for their service and no immediate prospects. Tall and massively built, bold and battle-tried, blessed with boundless energy and a burning ambition, it is not surprising that we next hear of Teach swaggering around in the pirate haven of New Providence, which boasted at that time a population of some 800 freebooters, including Benjamin Hornigold, on one of whose ships Teach got a berth, probably as mate, towards the end of 1716.

Their first cruise together was a success. Sailing north they took a sloop from Havana laden with flour, another out of Bermuda with a large cargo of wine, and a third from Madeira en route to South Carolina.

After a leisurely careen on the Virginia coast in the early spring, they turned south towards the Caribbean where they made prize of a large French Guineaman bound for Martinique. Teach, heaving his great bulk over the side, was first aboard the Guineaman, pistol in hand, cutlass gripped between his teeth. Resistance was negligible. He took an instant fancy to the ship and showed no inclination to leave her. Hornigold sized up the situation, tactfully appointed Teach captain of the prize, and sailed off. They were not to meet again.

Hornigold went back to New Providence where, with the arrival of Woodes Rogers, he received the King's Pardon, reformed completely and took to hunting pirates. His first commission from Rogers was to capture

Captain Teach

Charles Vane, reported to be on Green Turtle Cay, near Abaco. Hornigold found Vane — at least so he later declared — resting up on the low, sandy coral cay, and spent three weeks watching him from hiding, hoping to take him by surprise. Meanwhile Rogers began to have grave fears that Hornigold had discarded the Pardon and 'returned to the sport'. But he did come back, empty-handed, and Rogers was forced to admit to the Council of Trade: 'they failed in this'. Charles Vane was not taken that easily. Hornigold was later wrecked on a reef and drowned.

Teach, meanwhile, delighted with his new command, mounted her with forty guns, changed her name to the *Queen Anne's Revenge* and embarked on his own account. He was now beginning to earn a reputation for fury and wrath, for which he is chiefly remembered. He allowed his 'frightful meteor' of a beard to grow even longer and took to ranting into action armed to the teeth, carrying a sling over his shoulders with three brace of pistols hanging in holsters, like bandoliers.

He took a number of prizes, seeing their crews safely ashore before stealing or sinking their ships. He had a brisk fight with a thirty-gun British man-of-war, HMS *Scarborough*, which gave over the engagement after three hours and beat it back to her station at Barbados.

It was about May 1717 that Teach, making for that other pirate rendezvous in the Bay of Honduras, fell in with a ten-gun sloop commanded by a Major Stede Bonnet, one of the oddities of pirate history. The encounter was to have far-reaching results.

Bonnet — 'the Gentleman Pirate', as he came to be called — was a retired army officer of position and birth, who owned substantial property in Barbados where he had settled comfortably. Then suddenly, for no apparent reason, he decided to turn pirate. He bought a sloop, which no other pirate ever did, fitted her out at his own expense with ten guns and seventy men, called her the *Revenge* (a favourite name with pirates) and, one dark, moonless night, sailed from Barbados 'on the account'.

His friends were scandalized at first by his strange behaviour, but later sympathized with him when it was discovered that he had gone to sea to escape his wife's unbridled nagging!

Although new to seafaring and piracy, a fact quickly recognized by his crew to whom he was often forced to defer on important matters, Bonnet was successful enough at the start. He captured several ships off Virginia and the New England coasts from which he took much valuable loot, including provisions, clothing, money, ammunition and slaves, as well as rum and sugar (those essential ingredients of punch). He careened in a North Carolina inlet, probably close to Cape Fear River, then took the seas again for the Bay of Honduras where, as we have seen, he sailed into Teach's arms.

Teach looked the situation over with a practised eye, took Bonnet aboard his ship and put in one of his best men named Richards as captain of the major's sloop, apparently with the crew's consent. Johnson, probably not without a touch of irony, says Teach told Bonnet that as he had not been used to the fatigues and cares of such a post, it would be better for him to decline it and live easy, at his pleasure, in such a ship as his where he should not be obliged to perform duty, but follow his own inclinations! The major was far from pleased with the proposal, but had no choice, for the present at least.

This is a commonly accepted version of the story, but, in fact, Teach sailed in partnership with Bonnet for some time before the takeover. Walter Hamilton, governor of the Leeward Islands, writing on 6th January 1718 to the Council of Trade and Plantations from St Kitts where he had recently arrived after touring the Virgin Islands, reports that in the previous November Teach in his flagship and Bonnet in the sloop had taken a number of vessels belonging to St Kitts, as well as a Guadeloupe ship laden with white sugar which they sank just under the guns of Brimstone Hill! The report adds, strangely, that 'some say Bonnet commands both ship and sloop'. It is interesting that Hamilton, in his report, says that these depredations caused the people of St Kitts so much alarm for his safety in travelling from there to Antigua, that they impressed and manned a sloop to reinforce the small warship which was to see him up. One of the St Kitts vessels taken by Teach and company was the *Margaret*, Henry Bostock master. They took his cargo of cattle and hogs, his arms, books and instruments, but harmed none of his crew. Bostock was struck by the great deal of plate they had on board, especially by a very fine silver cup.

Continuing his cruise, as we left him, towards the Bay of Honduras, Teach stopped at Turneffe, a small island off the coast of Belize, to water, and, while there, surprised a ship coming in which struck at sight of Richards who had gone out to meet her in Bonnet's *Revenge*, and anchored meekly under the stern of Teach's vessel. She proved to be the *Adventure* sloop of Jamaica, David Harriot master. Teach took him and his crew aboard the great ship and put his own sailing master, Israel Hands, in charge of the sloop. Israel Hands, the source of Robert Louis Stevenson's character in *Treasure Island*, was to play an interesting role at the close of the Blackbeard drama.

After a week at Turneffe, Teach weighed and sailed into the Bay where they found a ship oddly named the *Protestant Caesar*, and four sloops, all of which surrendered at sight of Teach's black flag. Richards secured the sloops (one was burnt later to spite its owner for some undisclosed reason and the others were released) while Teach's quartermaster took possession of the *Protestant Caesar* which they plundered then burnt also because she belonged to Boston where a number of pirates had been hanged some six months before.

Teach now commanded a fleet of six vessels and some 400 men, including the unfortunate Stede Bonnet. There was his flagship the *Adventure*, the *Queen Anne's Revenge*, the *Revenge* filched from Bonnet, still under Richards' command, as well as a sloop and two smaller tenders. Sailing towards the low sandy island of Grand Cayman, about 175 miles west of Jamaica, he overhauled a small turtler – doubtless relieving her master of his catch of green turtles: a favourite pirate food – thence via Havana to the Bahama wrecks to hunt for sunken treasure from Spanish galleons that had foundered in the passage, a popular piratical pastime of the period.

Teach now sailed for South Carolina (taking a brigantine and a couple of sloops on the way) and towards the end of May lay off the entrance to Charleston harbour, a much-frequented hunting ground of the pirates. Well placed off the bar, he seized some nine prizes, including the *Crowley*, Captain Robert Clark, bound for England carrying a considerable sum in specie and a number of important passengers, including Samuel Wragg, a prominent Charleston citizen and member of the governor's Council, whom Teach held as a hostage. Meanwhile eight sail in the harbour ready for the sea did not dare venture out when it was learnt that Teach was off the bar. For the same reason, incoming ships now stayed away, bringing all trade to a standstill. Teach had effectively blockaded the port.

This was a great calamity, especially as the colony had just emerged from a long and bloody war with the Tuscarora Indian tribe which had proved costly in resources and manpower and left them in no position to cope with this formidable pirate infestation. Even so, worse was to come. Teach was, in fact, about to hold the colony to ransom!

Finding that his company was short of medicines, he sent Richards and some men ashore, and a passenger from the *Crowley* named Marks, to the governor Robert Johnson with a list of medical supplies he needed. He also sent a warning that unless the demand was met within a stated time he would destroy the vessels he had taken, put all the passengers to death – including Councilman Wragg – and 'come over the barr for to burn the ships that lay before the Towne and to beat it about [their] ears'.

On Marks' arrival the governor hastily convened a special meeting of the Council at which it was reluctantly agreed that in the circumstances they had no option but to comply with the pirate's demand. Accordingly a chestful of medicines (possibly, as has been suggested, mainly for the treatment of venereal diseases) valued at £400 was assembled and handed to Richards and his associates who, in the meantime, had been strutting with impunity about the streets of the town, watched by the angry, outraged citizens.

While on their way back to the ship with the medical supplies a squall upset their boat and Marks and the pirates had to put back to shore. By the time they got off again the following day, Teach's ultimatum had expired, but he did not carry out his fearful threat. He released the prisoners and the captured ships, having first helped himself to all the provisions and other useful items on board, as well as £1,500 in gold and silver, then sailed off towards North Carolina with his fleet.

News of Teach's exploits soon resounded up and down the coast of North America, as the anecdotes for which he was to be chiefly remembered began to be formed and the legends forged.

Drink and the Devil . . . Teach's drinking prowess and that of his crew became a byword and every seaman's dive echoed to the stories of his debauches. His journal is said by Johnson to have contained such entries as:

Such a day, rum all out: – Our company somewhat sober! – A damn'd confusion amongst us! – Rogues a-plotting: – Great talk of separation – so I looked sharp for a prize: – Such a day, took one, with a great deal of liquor on board, so kept the company hot, damned hot; then all things went well again.

As for the Devil, he encouraged his men in believing that he was either Old Nick himself or, at least, in close league with him. In the end he seems to have convinced himself that this was so! One day at sea, rather the worse for drink, he called some of the crew and said, 'Come let us make a hell of our own, and try how long we can bear it.' He then led them down into the hold, slammed all the hatches shut and set fire to several pots filled with brimstone and other inflammable stuff. Soon the men were coughing and gasping and crying out for air, while Teach danced around the hold, apparently unaffected by the fumes, roaring with laughter. His shipmates had almost suffocated to death when he kicked open the hatches and pushed them bodily out on deck, hugely pleased that he had endured 'hell' the longest.

Johnson records that on the night before he was killed, Teach sat up drinking with some of his men until dawn, when one of them discreetly asked, if anything should happen to him in the coming engagement, did his wife know where he had buried his money, to which Teach, leering evilly, answered that only he and the Devil knew where it was, and the longest liver should take all.

Johnson also tells the story, reputedly related by members of Teach's crew who were taken alive at the end, that once during a cruise they noticed that they had one man too many on board. He was seen for several days, sometimes below and sometimes up on deck, but no one seemed to know who he was or where he had come from, but all became convinced that the extra hand was the Devil himself. He disappeared as mysteriously as he had come.

Another of Johnson's stories concerns Teach's grisly sense of humour. Drinking below one night with Israel Hands and another man, Teach stealthily drew a small pair of pistols and cocked them under the table. The crewman saw the move and, excusing himself, made quickly for the deck as Teach, blowing out the candles, crossed the pistols and opened fire, hitting Hands in the knee and laming him for life. It was only a practical joke, of course, but when asked by his men why he had done it, he flew into a rage and damned them, saying that if he didn't kill one of them occasionally they would forget who he was! The bullet, as it happened, was to save Hands' life, but he never forgave Teach; he deserted him later, and got his own back, in the end.

But to return to Teach. We left him and his small fleet sailing up the coast towards North Carolina with its outer chain of long, narrow, barrier beaches and projecting capes. For some time he had been considering ways of breaking up his large company and securing most of the accumulated loot for himself, and now decided that the moment had come to act. Running into Topsail (now Beaufort) Inlet, north of Cape Fear, ostensibly to careen, he contrived to ground his ship. Israel Hands, who was probably privy to the plan, went to his assistance, running his sloop ashore also, close to his captain's. Teach then got into the tender with some forty of the crew, leaving the *Revenge* (which Bonnet soon resumed command of), and sailed away, marooning seventeen of the men en route on a barren, sandy cay some distance off. Bonnet managed to rescue the marooned men from certain death and chased after Teach, intent on avenging the indignities he had suffered at the other's hands, as well as the marooning of his men, but lost him. They were never to meet again.

Bonnet then made his way to Bath, at that time the capital of North Carolina, where he was granted the benefit of the King's Pardon by the governor, Charles Eden. Soon afterwards, however, he changed his sloop's name to the *Royal James*, his own to Thomas, and went 'on the account' once more, taking prizes off Virginia, Bermuda and Philadelphia! This doubtless caused little surprise. In Carolina the offer of pardon had actually proved an encouragement to pirates. There they came in, got their discharge, and probably disposed of some of their goods and effects; then, after a short holiday, went back to their former way of life. Bonnet was eventually cornered and captured near Cape Fear by the redoubtable Colonel William Rhett, Receiver-General of South Carolina, after a six-hour musketry duel. He was tried and hanged in Charleston. Rhett had gone out after Charles Vane but missed him. Vane meanwhile had sailed north and put in at Ocracoke Inlet where he had had his famous meeting with Teach. The trial of the gallant but unlucky Major Bonnet is remarkable for the inordinately long speech, crammed with biblical quotations, made by the trial judge Nicholas Trot. Bonnet is remembered not only for the unusual reason for his turning pirate, but also for the persistent, if unsubstantiated, story that he made his prisoners 'walk the plank'.

Like Bonnet, Teach had gone up to Bath and obtained his certificate of pardon from Governor Eden. The two, together with the Secretary Tobias Knight, were to become firm friends and close collaborators. This seemingly strange alliance between pirate and colonial official did not spring from any especial corruptness of the latter, as Patrick Pringle points out. The reason, he says, was that North Carolina was one of the few remaining places on the North American mainland where pirates were a blessing rather than a curse. This was the direct result of the Acts of Trade and Navigation which had been responsible for the welcome given to the pirates by most American colonies in the 1690s.

But times had changed since then. The New England colonies had lost interest in the pirates after the break-up of the Red Sea trade. South Carolina had developed her natural resources and, like Virginia, had a flourishing export trade – and therefore, again like Virginia, was hostile to pirates, but cordial to smugglers. For reasons of trade Robert Johnson, Governor of South Carolina, was just as strongly opposed to pirates as Governor Eden of North Carolina was friendly towards them.

One of the first favours Teach received from his influential friends was a clear title to his ship the *Adventure* which he had filched from her Spanish owners while pirating off Turneffe. She was condemned to Teach as lawful prize at a sitting of the Court of Vice-Admiralty, called especially for the purpose and presided over by Knight, even though Teach did not have a privateer's commission, England and Spain were at peace at the time anyway, and in fact the ship had belonged to a group of English merchants! Other dubious transactions of the kind were to follow.

About this time Governor Eden presided over Teach's marriage to a 16-year-old girl – his fourteenth wife, says Johnson, of whom perhaps a dozen were probably still living. From his base in Ocracoke Inlet, Teach would journey to the plantation where his young wife lived and after spending the night with her, 'It was his custom', Johnson assures us, 'to invite five or six of his brutal companions to come ashore, and he would force her to prostitute herself to them all, one after another, before his face.' So, at least, goes the story.

Soon Teach was on the move again, roving at will up and down the coast, as far north as Philadelphia, Pennsylvania, where the governor of the colony issued a warrant for his arrest, but was never able to serve it. Teach returned to North Carolina and sailed up the river to Bath with a cargo including some ninety slaves which he sold openly. Taking the seas once more in June 1718, reportedly on a trading voyage, he steered a course for Bermuda, meeting some English vessels on the way from which he took provisions and other necessaries. Near the island itself he fell in with two French ships bound for Martinique, one in ballast, the other laden with sugar and cocoa. He let the empty ship go, having transferred the crew of the other to her, and sailed back to Bath with his prize.

Going up to the governor, Teach and some of his men swore an affidavit that they had come on the French ship drifting out of control, without crew or papers. Once more a Court of Vice-Admiralty was called, with Tobias Knight again as judge, and the French ship was solemnly condemned as a wreck. For their cooperation in the matter, Governor Eden was rewarded with sixty hogsheads of the sugar and Knight twenty – gifts that were to prove a serious embarrassment to both men later.

But as long as the French ship remained afloat the affair was not at an end since she might at any time be recognized by the crew of some incoming vessel. Accordingly Teach gave it out that the ship was leaky and likely to go down at any time and so block part of the river. As a result he secured an order from the governor to burn and sink her, and with her sinking went any chance of her rising in judgement against them.

Teach does not seem to have sailed the high seas again, but spent several months operating from his base on the river, taking his ease in the coves or sailing from inlet to inlet, trading such plunder as he had with the sloops he met, and, when the mood took him, robbing them of their own cargoes.

He frequently went ashore to hobnob with the planter families. Johnson says:

By these he was well received, but whether out of love or fear, I cannot say. Sometimes he used them courteously enough, and made them presents of rum and sugar, in recompence of what he took from them; but as for liberties which, 'tis said, he and his companions often took with the wives and daughters of the planters, I cannot take upon me to say whether he paid them *ad valorem* or not. At other times he carried it in a lordly manner towards them; and would lay some of them under contribution; nay, he often proceeded to bully the Governor, not that I can discover the least cause or quarrel between them, but it seemed only to be done to show he dared do it.

But Teach's career was drawing to its close. It might have lasted longer, given the official patronage and support he enjoyed, had he been a more balanced and less egotistical person, but there was a limit to the insults and depredations the trading and commercial communities were prepared to endure.

South Carolina, weakened as it was, had had enough of the pirates and, as we have seen, succeeded in bringing in Stede Bonnet and his crew. Shortly after this Governor Johnson himself led an expedition against another notorious pirate captain, Richard Worley, who was lying off Charleston. After a fierce and bloody engagement in which twenty-six pirates were killed, Worley was captured with twenty-four of his men, tried and executed.

Realizing the futility of complaining to their own governor, a group of the more influential citizens of North Carolina appealed to Alexander Spotswood, the governor of Virginia, for help in ridding the colony of the Blackbeard menace. Spotswood was sympathetic and promised to do everything he could, especially when it was learnt in November that Teach was back in Ocracoke Inlet with a prize and preparing to fortify the shore and turn the place into 'another Madagascar'! A pirate rendezvous of the kind would pose a most dangerous threat to Virginian shipping.

Fortunately two British warships, the *Lyme* and the *Pearl*, were lying in the James River at the time as guardships and Spotswood conferred secretly with the captains on the action to be taken. He had not confided his plans to the Council for fear that word might get back to Teach since even here there was 'an unaccountable inclination to favour pyrates'. As it was impractical for the men-of-war to go into the shallows and difficult channels of Ocracoke Inlet, it was agreed that the governor would hire two small sloops, to be manned from the naval vessels. This was done and the command given to Lieutenant Robert Maynard of the *Lyme*, an experienced and, as events were to show, exceedingly courageous officer.

Although his position was juridically a delicate one, Spotswood managed to persuade the Council, shortly before the two sloops left, to pass an Act, on 14th November 1718, 'to Encourage the Apprehending and Destroying of Pirates'. Under this Act he was able to issue a Proclamation offering rewards for the taking of pirates 'within one hundred leagues of the Continent of Virginia, or within the Provinces of Virginia, or North Carolina'. This was an entirely irregular proceeding since Spotswood had no authority, legislative or otherwise, over another colony, but he was prepared to take the step. The Proclamation went on to set out the rewards offered: for the capture of Teach, dead of alive, £100; for every other commander of a pirate vessel, £40; for every lieutenant, master or quartermaster, boatswain or carpenter, £20; for other inferior officers, £15; and for every common crewman taken, £10.

On 17th November the two sloops stole out to sea, making their way south, stopping all vessels bound that way in order to keep the operation secret, but in vain, for word had got out and Teach had been warned by letter, on the governor's orders, from his devoted friend Tobias Knight. Even so, he had had other reports of the kind in the past which had turned out to be false alarms and so ignored this one, until the two sloops emerged out of the early evening coastal mists off Ocracoke Inlet.

Teach made a few desultory preparations for action, then, true to form, settled down to an all-night drinking bout. As dawn broke, Lieutenant Maynard weighed and sent his ship's boat ahead of the sloops to sound which, coming within gunshot of the pirate, received a heavy broadside, killing a number of navy men instantly, whereupon Maynard hoisted his colours and stood towards Teach. The latter cut his cable and tried to make a running fight of it, but ran aground. Maynard followed in his sloop, but was soon grounded also, being forced to heave ballast overboard to get free, then stood once more for him.

Seeing that the warship meant to run him aboard, the dreaded Blackbeard, in fearsome battle rig, his sword in hand, the six pistols primed and ready in their holsters, his plaited beard tossing in the wind and the lighted matches smoking from under his hat, lunged to the gunwale and hailing his pursuers called out, 'Damn you for villains, who are you?'

'You may see by our colours,' Maynard called back.

At which Teach, waving a bottle of rum, drank to the lieutenant, shouting: 'Damnation seize my soul if I give you quarter or take any from you!' To which Maynard answered that he expected no quarter from him, and would give none.

Teach's sloop now fell broadside to the shore and Maynard prepared to board. To prevent another slaughter of his men, Maynard had sent most of them below, holding the deck alone with the helmsman until the ships were alongside each other. Teach, seeing so few men on the other's deck and assuming that they had been all 'knocked on the head' by his broadside, tossed in some grenades made of case bottles packed with powder, small shot and slugs, with a quick match thrust into the mouth, then with fourteen of his crew swarmed over the vessel's bow, at which Maynard's men raced up on deck and engaged the pirates in a desperate hand-to-hand fight.

Teach and Maynard soon came face to face and a bloody duel followed. Although wounded by the lieutenant's first shot, Teach stood his ground and fought on with great fury, receiving, we are told, some twenty-five wounds, five of them by shot. He was in the act of cocking a pistol when he collapsed and died. None of his men yielded while they were in a condition to fight. Nine were killed, while navy casualties were ten killed and more than twenty wounded, some of whom later died. Teach had instructed a black crew member, a favourite of his, to blow up the sloop rather than let her be taken, but he never managed to do so.

Maynard sailed upriver to Bath to get help for his wounded men with Blackbeard's ghastly head dangling from the bowsprit end. He found a valuable cargo of sugar, cocoa, indigo and cotton in the holds of the pirate's sloop and came also on a number of incriminating documents among Teach's papers dealing with his relations with the governor and Mr Secretary Knight, including the guardedly worded warning of his (Maynard's) approach.

On the strength of this, Knight's barn was searched by Maynard and the sugar and cocoa with which he had been rewarded by Teach were seized. Later the governor's share was also confiscated. Six of Teach's crewmen, including Israel Hands, were tracked down in Bath, arrested and taken aboard the sloop in irons. The expedition then sailed back victoriously to Virginia with Blackbeard's head still bobbing up and down on the bowsprit end.

A good deal of legal wrangling was to follow, with much correspondence with London passing back and forth, and it was not until early the following year that Spotswood laid a full report of the affair before his

Council. The captured pirates were then tried in Williamsburg and thirteen of the fifteen hanged. Israel Hands turned King's evidence and eventually escaped the noose. His testimony threw some damning light on the relations between pirate Teach, Governor Eden and Tobias Knight.

No other pirate operated from a North Carolina base after the dreaded Blackbeard. His end, in fact, is regarded as virtually the end of American piracy.

Jack Rackham and the Women Pirates

With pitch and tar her hands were hard
Tho' once like velvet soft,
She weighed the anchor, heav'd the lead
And boldly went aloft.

Anon

It was a clear, sunny November day in the year 1720 when a trim pirate sloop, heeling to the fresh land breeze, rounded Negril Point on Jamaica's west coast and with magnificent impudence dropped anchor in the whitesand bay.

On the vessel's deck Captain Jack Rackham, better known as *Calico Jack* because of his penchant for calico underclothes, leaned against the breast-high gunwale and viewed the scene with a satisfied air. He had reason enough to be pleased. Battened down below decks was sufficient spoil for the present and adequate provisions for his crew. The sloop itself was a late contraband prize of the Don, filched by him in the best tradition of his trade. Even his search for crew replacements had been very successful. In the last ten days of October he had scoured every likely bay and cove on Jamaica's north side, drumming up recruits from the plantations so as to increase his company sufficiently for bigger work. He was lucky at Port Maria, but at Ocho Rios he had surprised a canoe which managed to elude his grasp and race for the safety of the shallows behind the low protective reef. Still, at Dry Harbour his luck had held again. Here he had found a ready supply of volunteers and here also he had overhauled a small sloop entering the beautiful half-moon bay as he was quitting it, relieved her of her cargo, and with admirable unconcern sailed slowly out of port.

Yes, Calico Jack had reason enough to be satisfied. With patience and cunning he had climbed the bloodstained rungs of the ladder of fame and the vista spread out before his gaze was fair to see. Of course his crew had helped him considerably. He always smiled slyly when he spoke of his crew. Such a crew! Not quite like any other, he always claimed . . . but he never explained what he meant.

No cloud dimmed the vision on that cool, clear November day. No warning shade from the future told of the shadows gathering even then on the horizon. It was good to be in this delightful place, good to be alive, good to be Jack Rackham. The occasion called for a celebration.

On shore a small group of people gathered at the waterside, anxious eyes and gestures turned often in the direction of the sloop riding the gentle groundswell with a slow, graceful roll. A piragua, gliding through the blue waters of the bay, made hastily for the shore at sight of the suspicious craft and ran on to the beach. Hailing the piragua's men Rackham bade them come aboard for a pipe of choice tobacco and a can of punch.

The piragua's crew, nine in all, hesitated for a while, then, seemingly reassured, put out again, tacked to larboard, drew up alongside the sloop and clambered aboard. The chances are that their thoughts were fixed more on the possibility of joining the pirate company than on the punchbowl but, as it happened, it would have been far better for them had they resisted the invitation, for they had no sooner joined the noisy party on deck than the white fleck of a sail appeared off the Point, growing swiftly larger against the sky's bright blue.

For weeks that sail had dogged the pirate's path. In his cruise along the north coast Rackham had lingered longer than a man of business ought to have, as was his tendency. The canoe which eluded him at Ocho Rios had carried news of his whereabouts to the governor, Sir Nicholas Lawes. Frustrated by the poor showing of the Navy against the pirates, Sir Nicholas had commissioned Captain Jonathan Barnet – 'a known and experienced Stout Brisk Man', in the words of a contemporary medical historian – and provided him with an armed sloop and instructions to patrol the island's coasts. No sooner did the news of Rackham's presence reach Lawes than he ordered Barnet in pursuit. Tenaciously Barnet had tracked his quarry from cove to cove, always one jump behind, until now, at last, he was drawing even.

In a moment the scene was changed aboard the pirate ship. Finding that the sloop stood directly towards him, Rackham immediately weighed and stood off, making a run for it. In answer to his shouted orders, the pipes and punchbowl were flung aside as all hands, including the men from the piragua, hurried to spread more and more canvas to the wind and, under the press of so much sail, the vessel buried her lee rails in the white foam and leapt lightly seawards.

Trim and swift as was the pirate ship, Barnet's craft, having the advantage of the freshening land breeze, began to outsail her. Relentlessly the hunter bore down on her quarry, the white wave rising to the thrust of her bows and spreading astern in a foamy wake. Even so, night had fallen before Barnet came within hailing distance. Asked what ship she was, a voice answered that she was commanded by Captain John Rackham of Cuba, at which Barnet promptly ordered that he should strike to the King of England.

'I'll strike no strikes!' Rackham roared back and defiantly opened fire. Barnet responded with a broadside, and using the time-honoured tactics of the pirates, ranged alongside the fleeing craft. From his vessel's deck grappling irons reached for the fugitive, and with drawn swords and pistols his sailors scrambled over the gunwales and on to the deck of the sloop.

The action that followed was bloody but brief. The pirates, still groggy from drink, lost heart early in the fight and gave ground before the determined onslaught of Barnet's men, fleeing to a vain retreat below decks. Two of their number only held their places, fighting shoulder to shoulder long after their comrades had retreated, fighting unaided against the whole of Barnet's crew. Had Rackham and the rest of his men shown half as much courage as these two members the issue would no doubt have been different. It is recorded that when the threats and curses of these two fiery freebooters failed to kindle the fuddled spirits of their comrades to a show of fight, one fired down the hold, killing a deserter outright and wounding others.

But even two pirates such as these are no match for a whole crew, and eventually they went down before the sheer weight of numbers and were captured. The sloop was quickly brought under control and manned, and the conflict ended with a strange suddenness as fate and the law finally caught up with Calico Jack Rackham and his notorious crew on that November day of the year 1720.

A fortnight later Captain Barnet sailed into Port Royal with the pirate sloop in close custody to receive the warm commendation of the government, as well as a reward of £200 – half for himself, the rest to be divided among his ship's company.

The news of Rackham's capture was startling enough, but even that was overshadowed when at a Court of Admiralty, held shortly after at St Jago de la Vega (the Spanish Town of today) and presided over by Sir Nicholas himself, the astonishing revelation was made that the two fire-eating filibusters who had staged the sensational last stand on the deck of the pirate were not men, but women disguised as men: Anne Bonny and Mary Read!

The story of these two sea-amazons is a remarkable one. Charles Johnson, to whom we are indebted for a full account of their lives, seems to have been himself acutely aware of the unbelievable nature of their biography. 'The odd incidents of their rambling lives are such', he writes, 'that some may be tempted to think the whole story no better than a novel or romance; but . . . it is supported by many thousand witnesses, I mean the people of Jamaica, who were present at their tryals, and heard the story of their lives, upon the first discovery of their sex.'

But the official report of their trial, which is our chief source of authentic documentary information, does not include the 'odd incidents' referred to by Johnson. These, in fact, were written up by him four years after the case was tried and perhaps, as Patrick Pringle thinks, may be 'as strange a blend of fact and fiction as that indefatigable historian ever concocted'.

In many particulars the lives of Anne and Mary are similar. Circumstances made it necessary for both to shed feminine identity at a tender age and adopt male manners and dress. They were both destined to sail under the Jolly Roger and, what was more remarkable, on the same ship, although it was but a short time before their famous last fight that each became aware of the other's true identity, in spite of the fact that for a long time they had both engaged in similar exploits.

Mary Read was born in England. Her mother, who married early, had a short married life. Soon after the wedding her young seafaring husband left England on a voyage from which he never returned, leaving her with a boy child, born some time after his departure.

The widow, who was 'young and airy', soon found herself faced with the prospect of having another child and with the difficulty of explaining satisfactorily how she had come by it. She solved her dilemma for a time by leaving London for the country where nobody knew her and where her second child, a girl whom she named Mary, was born.

She remained in the country for about four years, then, her slender resources exhausted, she found it necessary to return to London. It was then that fate took a hand. Her boy child died suddenly and she hit on the daring stratagem of dressing Mary in the boy's clothes and passing her off as her son.

The scheme worked well. Even Mary's grandmother was deceived and made her an allowance of a crown a week. Mary was only 13 when her grandmother died. This meant the end of the allowance and, with no other means of support, the girl was obliged to earn her own living.

Her first job was that of a 'footboy' to a French lady, but she quickly sickened of this service and, 'growing bold and strong, and having also a roving mind', she entered herself on board a British man-of-war. She soon tired of this also and deserted the sea for the army, joining a regiment of

Mary Read

foot in Flanders as a cadet, where her courageous behaviour won her the notice and esteem of her officers.

But Mary soon found herself falling in love with a young, handsome Fleming, her bedmate and constant companion in arms. Although she managed to conceal her passion she could not hide all the manifestations of that change that takes place in a woman in love. She became forgetful of army routine and negligent in the care of her weapons. These signs might have passed unnoticed but for her new habit of accompanying her companion, unordered, whenever he was dispatched on dangerous missions.

As the days went by her strange behaviour began to draw attention, and she was finding it increasingly difficult to hide her secret from the soldier himself. At length, says Johnson, 'As they lay together in the same tent, and were constantly together, she found a way of letting him discover her sex, without appearing that it was done with design.'

The Fleming's astonishment quickly gave place to keen delight at the discovery and he thought of little else but of gratifying his passion with scant ceremony. Mary, however, had other ideas, and he soon found himself courting her for a wife. When the campaign was over she publicly proclaimed her true identity and was married to her former comrade in arms, to the unbounded amazement and delight of the regiment, who subscribed liberally towards the couple's housekeeping.

They moved to Breda and there opened an eating-house called *The Three Horseshoes*, where they did a good business, their chief customers being the officers of their old regiment. But, as with her mother, Mary's married life was to be a short one. Her husband died suddenly and she was forced to close the eating-house.

Hedged round with difficulties she once again donned male clothing and returned to Holland where she joined a regiment of foot, forsaking the army later to take passage aboard a Dutch West Indiaman bound for the Caribbean. The vessel had the misfortune to be captured and plundered early on by an English pirate who, some accounts say, was Rackham himself. As the only English-speaking member of the crew Mary was offered a berth aboard the pirate ship (everyone believing her to be a man) which she readily accepted, becoming the second female crew member, although she did not know it at the time: her partner in disguise being none other than Anne Bonny!

Anne, like Mary, was an illegitimate child and Johnson gives what Pringle regards as a too blatantly invented pornographically circumstantial account of her conception. Her father was an attorney of County Cork, her mother his housemaid. The liaison which was to result in Anne's birth took place while the attorney's wife was spending time in the country for the benefit of her health.

She had suspected an affair between her husband and the maid, and on her return from the country concluded from certain signs that her suspicions were well founded. Her husband had not troubled himself to write to her once during her stay away and had gone out of town on the very day of her return on some slight pretext. Convinced that his reason for being away was in order to return during the night and spend it with the maid, she cunningly arranged for the latter to sleep elsewhere while she took her place in the bed.

'The husband came to bed, and that night play'd the vigorous lover', confides Johnson, 'but one thing spoiled the diversion on the wife's side, which was, the reflection that it was not design'd for her; however she was very passive, and bore it like a Christian.'

She appears to have been equally passive over the separation from her husband that not unreasonably followed. She was kinder to him than he deserved, for although they continued to live apart she made him a substantial allowance from her personal income.

It was some time later that the maid bore the attorney a daughter, whom he adopted. They called her Anne. To conceal its identity he dressed the child as a boy and said that it was a relative's son, but his wife had her doubts regarding the child, and discreet investigations revealed that it was not a boy at all but the maid's daughter. Unwilling to contribute towards its support, she immediately stopped her husband's allowance.

This was an ugly turn for the attorney who, realizing the futility of further pretence, defied convention and, taking the housemaid home, lived openly with her. His conduct soon became common talk and his practice fell off so sharply as a result that he was obliged to give up law. He moved to Cork where he stayed for a time before emigrating to Carolina, taking Anne and her mother with him. Once in America he soon forsook his legal profession for the more profitable life of a planter and in a short time became a prosperous plantation owner and a person of standing in the colony.

In spite of the amenities surrounding her upbringing, Anne grew into a strapping, boisterous girl whose fierce, ungovernable temper often got her into trouble. It is recorded that on one occasion she so thrashed a young

Anne Bonny

man who had made improper advances to her that he was laid up in bed for a considerable time.

The sea held a strong attraction for Anne and she fell into the habit of frequenting the waterfront disguised as a man. Her father, confident that she would outgrow her wayward habits, humoured her, setting about meanwhile to arrange a good match for her; but both his confidence and plans were to be rudely dashed one day when Anne turned up married to a shiftless seaman named John Bonny whom she had picked up in a waterside tavern. Turned out of doors by her exasperated parent, Anne and her sailor husband knocked about the seafront for a time, eventually making their way to New Providence.

It was about this time that the dashing Captain Jack Rackham also arrived in New Providence on a mission of repentance: he had come to claim the King's Pardon recently offered to all pirates who swore to eschew their old calling and settle down as decent, law-abiding citizens.

Rackham had by this time acquired a reputation as a fearless freebooter. In his early years he had served as quartermaster with Charles Vane's company aboard the *Independence*, but he was ambitious and promotion was not long in coming. It happened that one day a French man-of-war ran across the freebooters between Cuba and Hispaniola. She proved to be a very powerfully armed ship and Vane declined to engage her, much to his crew's disappointment. Rackham disputed Vane's decision, but the latter, says Johnson, 'made use of his power to determine this dispute, which, in these cases, is absolute and uncontrollable, by their own laws, viz. in fighting, chasing, or being chased . . . But the next day, the captain's behaviour was obliged to stand the test of a vote, and a resolution passed against his honour and dignity, branding him with the name of coward, deposing him from the command, and turning him out of the company.' With Vane went all those who did not vote for boarding the French man-of-war, and Rackham was unanimously chosen captain in his stead.

Not a great deal is known for certain about Rackham, outside the pages of Johnson, and there are inconsistencies in the stories which have come down to us. However, good fortune seems to have smiled on him from the start of his command. In his first cruise he took and plundered a number of vessels, including a Madeira ship en route to Jamaica, which took three days to loot. He had the goodness to return the ship to her master and arranged also for a Jamaican tavern keeper, Hosea Tisdale, whom he had picked up in another prize, to be given passage back to the island.

One of the strangest of his captures, perhaps, was a ship which turned out to be laden with convicts from Newgate prison, bound for service on the plantations – a grim sight which the pirates were no doubt glad to put out of their minds when she was retaken shortly afterwards by a British man-of-war.

But there were lean times too, and Rackham was rather down on his luck when the publication of the King's Pardon brought with it new hope. Making his way to New Providence about mid-May of the year 1719, he and some of his old cronies claimed the benefit of the amnesty. Selling the spoil he had with him for ready cash, the reformed pirate settled down on the island and abandoned himself to a life of ease and debauchery, for as long as his money should last.

Here the story becomes somewhat confused with two rather conflicting accounts given by the same source. However, it seems that it was shortly after his arrival that he ran into Anne Bonny. Anne, who had become the toast of the waterside taverns, was swept off her feet by the handsome, dashing freebooter whose methods of courting a woman and taking a ship were similar: no time wasted, straight up alongside, every gun brought to play, and the prize boarded.

The only hitch to their liaison was the regrettable existence of John Bonny. Anne, however, set about solving this difficulty with characteristic enterprise by approaching her husband for a formal separation, offering to have Rackham pay him a liberal sum by way of compensation. It is possible that John Bonny welcomed the arrangement. Anne had turned libertine on his hands and he had had little commerce with her since the day he caught her laying in a hammock with another man. But news of the business reached the ears of Governor Rogers through one Richard Turnley whom Anne had approached, unsuccessfully, to be a witness to the deed of separation. Anne and Rackham never forgave Turnley for what he did and tried later to corner him on a turtling cay, vowing to whip him to death since whipping, thanks to Turnley, was the punishment with which the governor had threatened her. Rogers had taken a serious view of the affair and summoned the parties concerned, giving them a piece of his mind together with the solemn promise that if he heard anything more about the proposed separation he would have Anne publicly flogged and Rackham himself would be made to wield the lash!

This was a grave disappointment to the couple. In addition Rackham had squandered all his gold and now began to feel the pinch of an empty pocket. Besides, life on shore was beginning to pall, especially if his love affair with Anne must now end, and he longed once again for the feel of a deck beneath his feet and the freedom of the blue Caribbean.

In Anne Bonny he found a kindred spirit. Between them they plotted secretly to seize a sloop which lay in the harbour and run away to sea. Rackham had no difficulty in gathering a crew of ex-pirates who like himself were fed up with shore life and longed to be back 'on the account'. He readily agreed to take Anne along, of course, provided she disguised herself as a man (no new departure for her) and swore to keep her identity secret.

The sloop they fixed on was between thirty and forty tons, one of the swiftest sailers ever built. She belonged to a John Haman who lived with his family on one of the Bahama islands, not far from Providence, from which he preyed on Spanish vessels plying between Cuba and Hispaniola, always managing to elude capture chiefly by virtue of the swiftness of his sloop, so much so that it became a saying in those parts: 'There goes John Haman, catch him if you can.'

After some smart spying ably done by Anne, a date was fixed for the venture, the time midnight. Fortune was kind to the schemers, the night was dark and rainy, all hands were punctual, and, with Anne Bonny back in male clothes the most resolute of the lot, they took a boat and rowed out to the sloop. Once on board, Anne, armed with sword and pistol, surprised the ship's watch and convinced them that silence was their best policy. Rackham and the others meanwhile hastily heaved in one cable, slipped the other and drove down the harbour.

They had to sail past the fort and the guardship, which hailed them, asking where they were going. Through the fog and rain Rackham called back that his cable had parted and there was nothing on board but a grappling which would not hold them. Shrouded by the darkness he put out one small sail to give them steerage way, then, once past the harbour mouth, up to the sloop's tapering spars rose sail after sail as the swift vessel bounded out into the night and loud cheers broke from the throats of the pirate crew. It was on the deck of this sloop, presumably, that the paths of the two women pirates at last converged, and there one of the strangest chapters in West Indian pirate history was to be written.

From then on Rackham's fame and success owed much to the daring and prowess of his two female crew members who, although unaware of each other's secret, became close friends and always went into action side by side. This strange attraction eventually led to a mutual revelation of their real selves for Anne, falling in love with Mary whom she took for a handsome young seaman, first told the other the secret of her sex. 'Mary Read,' says Johnson, 'knowing what she would be at, and being very sensible of her own incapacity that way, was forced to come to a right understanding with her, and so to the great disappointment of Anne Bonny, she let her know she was a woman also.'

Rackham, meanwhile, noticing the growing intimacy between Anne and the young sailor, threatened to cut the latter's throat if the affair continued, thus forcing Mary to take him also into her confidence which, to the end, he never betrayed.

Romance was to enter Mary Read's life once more before the curtain fell on her masquerading career. On their cruise the freebooters took and plundered a number of ships out of Jamaica, on board one of which was a young fellow of a most engaging behaviour whom Rackham pressed into service aboard his sloop.

It was not long before the newcomer had unwittingly won Mary's heart. They soon became messmates and close companions and Mary prepared her plans for making her true identity known to him. 'When she found he had a friendship for her, as a man,' Johnson records, 'she suffered the discovery to be made, by carelessly showing her breasts, which were very white.'

The days that followed were wildly happy for the couple. They pledged their troth to each other and lived as husband and wife. This, Mary later declared before a Jamaican court, she looked upon to be as good a marriage in conscience as if it had been done by a minister in church.

An unexpected turn of events, however, was soon to cast a shadow over their happiness and give Mary the chance to demonstrate the depth and selflessness of her devotion. It happened that the young seaman quarrelled one day with another crew member who challenged him to a duel. The sloop being at anchor off one of the islands, the two men appointed an hour when they should go ashore and settle their dispute, swords and pistols, pirate fashion.

Mary was frantic with anxiety when she learnt of the impending duel and determined to prevent it at all costs. Accordingly she took the first opportunity possible to start a quarrel with the pirate and, challenging him ashore, fixed the time two hours earlier than that at which he should meet her lover.

Mary Read had fought duels in her time, but never before from such a motive or with so fierce a determination to win. At the appointed time she and the pirate went ashore and together selected a secluded spot for their fight. Their exchange of fire resulted in no hits on either side and, whipping out their cutlasses, they began the duel to the death.

The pirate was heavier and stronger than Mary, but in her he found an adversary quick and agile, who was able to parry or elude his every stroke. Back and forth across the beach they fought, their blades clashing with sharp staccato notes, their footsteps weaving the pattern of conflict in the soft, white sands of the cay.

The pirate, heavier and slower than his opponent, began to tire first. Beads of sweat glistened on his hairy face and his breath now came with effort. Gradually through the haze of hate clouding his mind broke the cold realization that his antagonist was trifling with him, wearing him out against the instant when he should relax his guard . . .

Summoning all his strength he lunged at Mary in a fierce and desperate offensive, but she had danced beyond his reach whilst he, carried forward by the savagery of his attack, lost his balance for a moment. He would no doubt have recovered but for his opponent who leapt to his side and in one quick motion tore open her rough sailcloth shirt. For an instant only the pirate forgot his guard, forgot his peril as he stared in utter astonishment at what he saw. But that instant was his undoing, for Mary, grasping his sword arm, almost severed his head with a stroke of her cutlass. The pirate crumpled slowly sidewards to the ground, his fingers clutching convulsively, a red foam bubbling from his lips, staining the white sands of the cay.

Suddenly Mary Read heard the familiar sound of a boat grounding on the beach and looked up, smiling. It was her lover, come in good time to keep his appointment with the pirate.

But to return to Rackham's story, he was, as we have already seen, a man of undoubted personal courage and initiative, but with a rather reckless streak which often led him to linger too long in uncertain circumstances, as the following incident shows. After his escape from New Providence, he cruised about for a while then made for a favourite cove on the Cuban coast where he kept 'a little kind of a family', and where he and the crew spent a considerable time, living it up with their doxies and drink. The interlude over, he was making ready for sea again when in sailed a Spanish *guarda costa*, with an English sloop captured on the coast, which at once opened fire. Rackham's position, in a narrow channel close in behind a little island, saved him from immediate destruction, but, bottled up as he was, there seemed no hope of escape, and as the short West Indian twilight changed to night, the Spaniard warped into the channel to make sure of his capture the following day.

But Jack Rackham had been in tight spots before and he soon devised a way to cheat the Don. He waited until the dead of night when, lowering one of his ship's boats, he placed his crew with their weapons in her, and with muffled oars rowed round the island unnoticed by the Spaniards. There he found the English prize lying for better security close in to the land and silently they boarded her, threatening the Spanish prize crew with instant death if they so much as made a sound. He then slipped her cable and drove out to sea. As day broke the Spanish man-of-war opened a furious bombardment on what they were soon to discover was an empty vessel!

Once more Rackham's resourcefulness had come to his rescue, but as we pick up his story in August 1720, we learn of him in poor circumstances, reduced to running at low game, largely because of a shortage of hands. Still, there were some successes to come, before that fatal landfall on Jamaica's west coast.

By early September he had captured seven or eight fishing boats near Harbour Island from which he took nets and tackle, then making his way to the French part of Hispaniola he seized some cattle to replenish the food supply, and collared a couple of French hunters as well whom he forced to join his crew. On the way to Jamaica in early October he secured a couple of sloops from which he took tackle and apparel valued at £1,000, while off Port Maria he captured the schooner belonging to the unlucky Thomas Spenlow, plundered by other pirates only a few months before, and relieved her of fifty rolls of tobacco and some bags of pimento. Rackham then continued his leisurely cruise along the island's north coast which was to end sadly in Negril Bay.

Among the Colonial Office records, in the Public Record Office, London, is a rare pamphlet printed in Jamaica by Robert Baldwin who set up the island's first printing press (see opposite).

As the actual Admiralty Court records relating to the trial no longer exist, this pamphlet is of supreme importance for the story of Rackham and the women pirates. Nor can there be any question of its authenticity since it was sent to the Council of Trade and Plantations in lieu of a written official report by the governor Sir Nicholas Lawes, who himself presided over the court.

It furnishes no information about the previous history of the two women beyond the description of them as 'late of the Island of *Providence* Spinsters', nor on certain points does it substantiate Charles Johnson's account, but this is doubtless explained by his own admission that he included 'some

THE
TRYALS
OF
Captain John Rackam,
AND OTHER
PIRATES, *Viz.*

Geroge Fetherſton,	Noah Harwood,
Richard Corner,	James Dobbins,
John Davies,	Patrick Carty,
John Howell,	Thomas Earl,
Tho. Bourn, *alias* Brown,	John Fenwick, *al'* Fenis

Who were all Condemn'd for PIRACY, *at the Town of* St. Jago de la Vega, *in the Iſland of* JAMAICA, *on* Wedneſday *and* Thurſday *the Sixteenth and Seventeenth Days of* November 1720.

AS ALSO, THE

TRYALS *of* Mary Read *and* Anne Bonny, *alias* Bonn, *on Monday the* 28th *Day of the ſaid Month of* November, *at* St. Jago *de la Vega aforeſaid.*

And of ſeveral Others, who were alſo condemn'd for PIRACY.

ALSO,

A True Copy of the Act of Parliament made for the more effectual ſuppreſſion of Piracy.

Jamaica : Printed by *Robert Baldwin*, in the Year 1721.

particulars which were not so publicly known', while in support of those who question Johnson's impersonation story is the evidence given in court against the women pirates by two Frenchmen – John Besneck and Peter Cornelian who claim to have been captured and forced by Rackham – that 'when they saw any vessel, gave chase, or attacked, they wore men's clothes; and, at other times, they wore women's clothes'.

The *other PIRATES* of the pamphlet include Rackham's nine guests from the piragua. Lovat Fraser in his book *Pirates* (1921), says that the judge, in passing sentence of death on them, made a very pathetic speech, exhorting them to bear their sufferings patiently, assuring them that if they were innocent, which he very much doubted, then their reward would be greater in the Other World. But, adds Mr Fraser, everybody must own their case was very hard in this. The judge's speech is, unfortunately, not recorded in the Baldwin pamphlet.

Rackham was hanged at Gallows Point, on the Palisadoes, his body being later squeezed into a 'suit of iron' and gibbeted on the sandy cay off Port Royal which bears his name today, as a warning to the piratically-minded. Scaffolds and gibbets cost at that time £40 and suits of iron £9 apiece. On the morning of his execution he was allowed, as a special favour, a visit from his sweetheart of happier days. The meeting was short and disappointing for the condemned pirate chief; the fiery Anne, still outraged at his conduct off Negril, had no word of consolation for him. She said she was sorry to see him there, 'but if he had fought like a man, he need not have been hanged like a dog'.

When their sex was discovered in court, Anne Bonny and Mary Read were ordered a separate trial. This was held on 28th November, over a week after Rackham and the rest had been executed. The evidence mustered against the women pirates was heavy. It included the deposition of one Dorothy Thomas whose canoe was plundered by Rackham during his cruise along the north coast. She said it was the largeness of their breasts which betrayed their real sex to her woman's eye, for otherwise they wore men's jackets and trousers, tied their heads with handkerchiefs and each carried a cutlass and pistol. She said they cursed and swore at the men to kill her to prevent her 'coming against them' later.

Another witness, Thomas Dillon, master of a sloop taken by the pirates, said that Anne and Mary were both 'very profligate, cursing and swearing much, and very ready and willing to do anything on board'.

To these and other charges the women pirates offered nothing material by way of answer. They were found guilty, of course, and sentenced to death. But as soon as judgement was pronounced both women informed the court that they were pregnant and prayed that execution of the sentence might be stayed! An 'inspection' ordered by the court later confirmed the truth of their plea and their sentence was accordingly respited.

Both cheated the gallows, in the end. Anne was reprieved from time to time and disappears from recorded history, although it is believed that her father, through his connections with influential planters in the island with whom he had dealt, arranged for her return to Carolina; while Mary died of fever contracted during her lying-in. Her burial on 28th April 1721 is briefly recorded in the earliest Parish Register of Burials of St Catherine.

Mary's lover was acquitted as the evidence in court (much of it provided by Mary) proved that he had been pressed into service aboard the pirate sloop. According to Johnson, Mary herself might have earned the clemency of the court but for one damning piece of evidence. It was disclosed that on being asked once what profit she could find in a life continually threatened by death from fire, sword or hanging, she replied that 'as to hanging, she thought it no great hardship, for, were it not for that, every cowardly fellow would turn pirate, and so infest the seas, that men of courage must starve'. A fitting epitaph for the women pirates of the West Indies.

Captain John Evans

Some pirates had talent and outstanding success but short and tragic careers. Such a one was the Welshman Captain John Evans. We pick up his story around 1722, a bad time for seafarers of his ilk with berths scarce and wages low.

He had been master of a Nevis sloop but lost the job and sailed for a time as mate out of Jamaica. Angry and frustrated at conditions, he and three or four cronies decided to go 'on the account'. Getting hold of a canoe they rowed out of Port Royal towards the end of September 1722, travelling around the island, putting in at night in small bays and creeks, robbing and looting houses as they went, but hoping all the time that 'providence would send some unfortunate vessel as a sacrifice'.

At Duns Hole, St James, a few miles east of Montego Bay, near the Little River, they found what they needed so badly – a small sloop belonging to Bermuda. They promptly boarded it and Evans announced grandly that he was the new captain and that the vessel now belonged to him and his men, which, says Johnson, 'was a piece of news they knew not before'.

In an expansive gesture Evans and his crew then went ashore to a little village where they drank heartily and enjoyed themselves at the local tavern so much that the owner and his people were mightily pleased with their merry guests and wished for their company another time.

This came sooner than they expected: that very midnight, in fact, when Evans and his party returned, raided and robbed the place of everything of value, loaded the loot aboard the sloop – now renamed the *Scowerer* and mounting four guns – and weighed anchor at daybreak.

They sailed to Hispaniola where, on the north side, they soon took a Spanish sloop. She proved to be a profitable prize from which each man got about £150. Beating up for the Windward Islands the *Scowerer* met a New England ship off Puerto Rico, the 120-ton *Dove* bound for Jamaica, and plundered her, taking the mate and two or three other men before releasing their prize.

Other ships fell prey to the pirate, including the *Lucretia and Catherine* of

200 tons which Evans took with him to the island of Aves intending to use her for heaving down the *Scowerer* in order to scrape and clean her bottom, but other likely prizes crossed the pirate's path and careening was forgotten for the chase.

Eventually, back again off the coast of Jamaica, Evans took a sugar droger, then ran for nearby Grand Cayman in order to careen his ship, but here the short and profitable career of Captain John Evans was to end, tragically, as so many others did.

It happened that the ship's boatswain was a noisy, ill-natured man with whom Evans had had to remonstrate often. Now, however, as the sloop approached the island, matters came to a head with the boatswain challenging Evans to a duel ashore, swords and pistols, pirate fashion.

But at the appointed time the boatswain lost heart and to everyone's astonishment refused to leave the ship or fight. When Evans saw there was nothing to be done with him, he seized his cane and began to thrash him thoroughly, but the boatswain drawing a pistol shot Evans dead, then leapt overboard intending to swim to shore.

The outraged crew quickly lowered a boat, caught up with the fugitive and brought him back to the ship. They decided that he should die by the most exquisite tortures, but while considering the form of punishment the forthright gunner shot him through the body, another crewman finishing him off with a bullet in the head.

The *Scowerer*'s company now found themselves in a serious difficulty as their only navigator was the mate whom they had pressed into service early on. They now offered him the command of the sloop, but he firmly declined, so it was decided to leave the vessel in his possession and break up the company, the thirty crewmen going ashore at Grand Cayman with some £9,000 to divide among them.

Fortunately the weather held fair and in due course the mate and a boy managed to sail the *Scowerer* safely back to Port Royal.

Nicholas Brown, the 'Grand Pirate'

As Captain Evans' men walked away into the sunset, so to speak, to vanish from history, the sun was in fact setting on the great age of piracy. The outbreak of the War of the Spanish Succession played its part, but more important perhaps was the effective enforcement of the law and one of the most energetic enforcers was Sir Nicholas Lawes, the then governor of Jamaica who, as we have seen, was responsible for bringing in Jack Rackham and his extraordinary crew.

Another notorious pirate of this period whom Lawes tried hard to get his hands on was Nicholas Brown – known in his day as the 'Grand Pirate' – and his companion Christopher Winter. As it happened, Lawes did not have the satisfaction, but Brown was to come to an unpleasant end just the same.

In 1718 Brown had accepted the King's Pardon at New Providence in the Bahamas, together with some 150 others, including such big names in the pirate round as Blackbeard, Benjamin Hornigold and Edward England. But, as Johnson says, 'the greatest part of them returned again, like the dog to the vomit', including Brown and Winter who surrendered shortly afterwards to the governor of Cuba and enjoyed his shelter and support.

We next hear of Brown attacking a- ' plundering English ships along Jamaica's north coast, stealing slaves from the plantations and, on one occasion, burning down a house in St Ann with sixteen people, including children, trapped inside.

The news of this atrocity shocked the island. The House of Assembly called for rewards to be offered for the capture of Brown and his companion Winter, but the governor asked the members bluntly, where the money was to come from? The island's finances were in a bad way, the Treasury was empty, and no one knew that better than Sir Nicholas whose salary was already two years in arrear.

All the same, something had to be done. Rewards were effective. They had worked in Rackham's case, so the money was found somehow – a

£500 reward for the capture of Brown and £300 for Winter. In the meantime, however, the governor decided to try diplomatic channels.

He dispatched a Captain Chamberlain, commander of the snow HMS *Happy*, with a letter dated 26th January 1721, to the 'Alcades of Trinidado on Cuba', complaining of the frequent depredations and other acts of hostility, done with their connivance and support, and, surprisingly, at a time when peace and amity subsisted between their two nations. He demanded satisfaction for the many notorious robberies committed, particularly by 'those Traytors, Nicholas Brown and Christopher Winter' and insisted that they deliver up to the bearer such Englishmen as were now detained or otherwise remained in Trinidado.

The Alcaldes' reply to this, and a further letter delivered by Captain Joseph Lawes (no relation of the governor), was a model of smooth diplomacy. They wished to state, it said, that there were no negroes or vessels in their city or port taken at Jamaica since 'the Cessation of Arms', and as for those English fugitives, 'they are here as other subjects of Our Lord the King, being brought voluntarily to our Holy Catholic Faith, and have received the Water of Baptism'.

And that was the end of the affair. Meanwhile in Jamaica anger was growing, as well as interest in the rewards being offered for the two pirates. Among the people who took a particular interest in the matter was a certain John Drudge, captain of the sloop *Portland*. As he studied the heavy-printed notices of the reward, stuck up about the town, his mind probably went back to the time when he and Nicholas Brown attended the same small school at Port Royal, run by Mercy Moore. How different the future had seemed then! He doubtless wondered what it was that had changed the boy he remembered Brown to have been into the mad dog of today, with blood on his hands and a price on his head, hunted wherever he went.

And he, John Drudge, would join the hunt. Brown was dangerous, but his capture was worth £500. The question was, where should he begin to look for the 'Grand Pirate'? He was to wait six years for the answer.

It happened that on 18th October 1726 Drudge and his sloop *Portland* sailed from Jamaica for the South Cays of Cuba where, on arrival on 2nd November, he anchored at the barkadeer of Santa Cruz del Sur on the mainland. Two Dutch vessels had arrived there before him. A group of merchants of Puerto Príncipe (now Camagüey) had sent letters saying that they were willing to trade if it could be guaranteed that they and their goods would be protected against attacks by pirates. Drudge supplied twenty well-armed men from his crew who were reinforced by ten others from the Dutch ships. He ordered them to set off at three the following morning to escort the merchants. The Dutchmen complained at first about having to get up so early, but Drudge was not a safe man to argue with and, as he himself says, 'he ordered them about their business'.

As feared, the party ran across some thirty-five pirates when only five miles inland on the savanna. They tried to bypass them but were spotted and a skirmish developed which ended with Drudge's men racing back to the barkadeer, in defiance of strict orders to the contrary. Next morning, at sunrise, Drudge spied several men scrambling to get into two small piraguas within gunshot and ordered his party in pursuit, but there was almost a mutiny as the men flatly refused to obey; what was more, they also refused to go in search of those wounded in the engagement of the day before. Eventually Drudge offered a reward of fifty pieces-of-eight for every Englishman or Dutchman recovered, but he was able to tempt only one volunteer—William Ledbetter of Port Royal—who set off across the savanna, accompanied by two Spanish hunters. Some hours later the trio returned with three of the wounded – two Spaniards and another man who to John Drudge's surprise and keen delight proved to be none other than his old schoolmate, Nicholas Brown, the 'Grand Pirate'.

Drudge was so pleased with the hunters that he gave them an extra 120 pieces-of-eight as reward. He could afford to: £500 awaited him in Jamaica for Brown's capture, £500 current money of the island, a small fortune, and Drudge needed it badly.

But there was one snag: Brown had been badly wounded in the right arm and was half-dead from shock and loss of blood; what was more, gangrene had set in. Drudge sent for the Dutch doctors to come aboard his ship and a consultation was held. There was only one thing to do: amputate the arm. It was grim, but it had to be done. Drudge plied his scarcely conscious ex-schoolmate with neat rum to help cushion the pain and shock, then the surgeons took over.

The operation, done on 20th November, was not a complete success. Five days later, as Drudge's sloop was off Port Maria on Jamaica's north coast, Brown died. This raised another problem for Drudge since he could not possibly keep the dead body long enough to establish his right to the reward, but he soon thought of a way out. He hacked off Brown's head with a cutlass, popped it into a keg of rum and dumped the decaying body overboard for the sharks.

When John Drudge appeared before the House of Assembly in Spanish Town on 3rd March the following year to demand the £500, questions were asked as to the genuineness of his claim. He made a suitable deposition and informed the members that the pickled head of his notorious captive was even then in the office of Mr Sebran Larson, deputy marshal for St Catherine, where it could be viewed – but none of the members of the Honourable House seemed inclined to pursue the matter. The 'Grand Pirate' was formally deemed dead and John Drudge received his reward.

Date Chart

Events in the Caribbean from the arrival of Christopher Columbus to the War of American Independence

1492	Christopher Columbus discovers the New World
1506	French ships operating in the Caribbean
1542	The Dutch trading in the Caribbean
1562–68	John Hawkins' four trading voyages
1573/1585	Francis Drake's exploits in the Caribbean
1615	Court of Vice-Admiralty set up in Newfoundland
1624	St Kitts settled by the English
1627	Barbados settled by the English
1628	Nevis settled by the English
1630	Buccaneers move from their original base in Hispaniola to Tortuga
1632	Antigua and Montserrat settled by the English
1635	Henry Morgan born
1651	Navigation Act passed
1652–54	First Dutch War
1655	Jamaica captured from Spain by the English
1660	Navigation Act passed
1664–71	Sir Thomas Modyford governor of Jamaica
1665–67	Second Dutch War
1667	Edward Mansfield, buccaneer leader, dies; is succeeded by Henry Morgan
1668–69	Henry Morgan sacks Puerto Príncipe, Porto Bello and Maracaibo
1668–71	Some 2,600 men from Jamaica join the buccaneers
1670	Henry Morgan sacks Panama
	Treaty of Madrid signed, concluding peace between England and Spain
1671	Governor Modyford replaced by Sir Thomas Lynch and sent as a prisoner to England to answer for the sacking of Panama, but is later sent back to Jamaica
1672	Henry Morgan sent to England for the same reason, but is later knighted and sent back to Jamaica

1672–74	Third Dutch War
1674	⎫
1678	⎬ Sir Henry Morgan lieutenant-governor of Jamaica
1680–82	⎭
1678–80	Earl of Carlisle governor of Jamaica
1680	A group of buccaneers, including Richard Sawkins, launch the Pacific Venture
1681–82	Rev. Lancelot Blackburne, later Archbishop of York, sails with the buccaneers
1682	Bartholomew Roberts born
1688	Sir Henry Morgan dies
1688–97	War of the Grand Alliance, ended by the Treaty of Ryswyck
1692	Great earthquake at Port Royal, Jamaica
1694	French force attack Jamaica; defeated at Carlisle Bay
1696	Navigation Act passed
1702–13	War of the Spanish Succession, ended by the Treaty of Utrecht
1716	Edward Teach ('Blackbeard') takes to piracy
1716–26	Some 600 Anglo-American pirates executed
1718–22	Sir Nicholas Lawes governor of Jamaica
1718	Edward Teach killed
	Woodes Rogers arrives in the Bahamas as governor, Act of Pardon passed
	Richard Worley and Howel Davis take to piracy
1719	Bartholomew Roberts takes to piracy
1720	Charles Vane and Jack Rackham hanged
	Mary Read dies in prison in Jamaica
1721	George Lowther takes to piracy
1722	Bartholomew Roberts killed; he had captured some 400 ships during his career
	John Evans takes to piracy
	Forty-one pirates hanged in Jamaica
1722–26	Duke of Portland governor of Jamaica
1723	Finn and five pirates hanged in Antigua; eleven others hanged there later
1726	Nicholas Brown dies
1776	Outbreak of the War of American Independence

Glossary

account, to go on the   to embark on a piratical cruise.

Acts of Pardon, or of Grace   general amnesties under which a reformed pirate might surrender in return for a certificate of pardon.

Acts of piracy   acts for the establishment of *Vice-Admiralty Courts* and the suppression of piracy.

ballast   heavy material used to stabilize a vessel, especially one not carrying cargo.

barkadeer   a small pier or jetty.

barque   a sailing ship of three or more masts having the foremasts rigged square and the aftermast rigged fore-and-aft.

'bilged upon her anchor'   holed or pierced by the ship's own anchor.

booms, or fenders   spars to which a sail is fastened to control its position relative to the wind.

boot-topping   a hurried, partial *careen*.

bowsprit   a spar projecting from the bow of a vessel used to carry the headstay as far forward as possible.

brig, brigantine   a two-masted sailing ship, rigged square on the foremast and fore-and-aft with square topsails on the mainmast.

'brought a spring upon her cable'   came round in a different direction.

brûlot   (French) a *fireship*.

buccaneers   the original 'cow killers' who settled illegally on Hispaniola, and who were so called for their method of smoke-curing meat on a *boucan*. Later, in the seventeenth and eighteenth centuries, they took to the sea and preyed on Spanish colonies and shipping in America and the Caribbean.

capstan   a windlass with a vertical drum, used for hauling in ropes, etc.

careen, to   to cause a vessel to keel over on its side in order to clean or repair its bottom.

careenage   a careening place.

chase guns   cannon situated at the bow of a ship, used during pursuit.

chequeen   sequin, a former Venetian gold coin.

clap in irons, to   to chain.

corsair see *pirate*.
crimp a person who swindled or pressganged seamen.

dory a fisherman's dugout.
doubloon a former Spanish gold coin.
droger a West Indian coasting vessel.

Execution Dock the usual place for pirate hangings, at Wapping Old Stairs on the Thames, in London.

filibuster see *freebooter*.
fireship a vessel loaded with explosives and used as a bomb by igniting it and directing it to drift among an enemy's warships (see *brûlot*).
flota (Spanish) a fleet.
flotilla a small fleet.
flying-jib the jib set furthest forward or outboard on a vessel with two or more jibs.
freebooter (filibuster) another name for a buccaneer or pirate.

galleon a large sailing ship having three or more masts latine-rigged on the aftermasts and square-rigged on the fore- and mainmasts, used either as a warship or for trade.
galley a low, flat-built vessel, propelled partly or wholly by oars.
gibbet a wooden structure resembling a gallows, from which bodies of executed pirates were hung to public view.
grapple, or grapnel a hooked instrument thrown with a rope for gripping and closing with an enemy's ship.
grenade these were made from square-faced case bottles, filled with gunpowder, small shot, bits of old iron, and thrown by hand.
guarda costa a vessel fitted out in Spanish or colonial ports and commissioned by local governors to enforce Spain's trade monopoly.
guineaman a ship engaged in the slave trade on the Guinea Coast of West Africa.

heave down, to to turn a vessel on its side for cleaning.
hogshead a large cask used mainly for shipment of wines and spirits.

interloper an illegal trader.

jack a flag, especially one flown at the bow of a ship to indicate her nationality.
Jolly Roger the pirate flag.

King's Pardon see *Acts of Pardon*.

larboard   the left (or port) side of a vessel when facing the bow.

Letters of Marque or Reprisal   commissions or licences to fit out armed vessels to be employed in the capture of enemy merchant shipping and to commit other hostile acts which would otherwise be condemned as piracy.

mainsheet   the line used to control the angle of the mainsail to the wind.

man-of-war   a warship.

maroon, to   to put ashore and abandon a person on a barren island or cay.

marooners   a name sometimes given to pirates because of their use of marooning as a form of punishment.

moidore   a former Portuguese gold coin.

patarero   a kind of muzzle-loading mortar which fired scattering shot, stones, spikes, old nails, broken glass, etc.

piece-of-eight   a former Spanish coin.

pinnace   any of various kinds of ship's tender.

piragua   a type of native dugout canoe.

pirate   a sea robber.

press (or force)   to recruit for naval or military service by forcible means.

privateer   a privately owned, armed vessel operating under *Letters of Marque*.

purchase   payment in the form of loot, as in the expression 'no purchase [or prey] no pay'.

quarter   mercy shown to a defeated opponent. A **ship's quarter** is that part of a vessel's side towards the stern, usually aft of the aftermost mast.

road   a partly sheltered anchorage.

salmagundy (salmagundi)   a dish of chopped meat, eggs, anchovies, onions, etc.

schooner   a sailing vessel with at least two masts with all lower sails rigged fore-and-aft.

sea artist   sailing master.

sloop   a single-masted vessel rigged fore-and-aft with a long bowsprit, much favoured by the pirates because of its shallow draught and manoeuvrability.

smack   a sailing vessel usually sloop-rigged, used in coasting or fishing.

snow   a small sailing vessel, resembling a brig, carrying a main- and foremast and a supplementary trysail mast close behind the mainmast.

Spanish Main   the mainland of Spanish America, from the Isthmus of Panama to the present republics of Colombia and Venezuela.

spike (guns)   to render a gun useless by blocking the vent or touch-hole with a spike, often a soft nail.

A snow

spritsail-yard   a yard (or one of several) set on the underside of the bowsprit, to carry a spritsail.

starboard   the right side of a vessel when facing the bow.

strike (colours)   to haul down a ship's flag as a signal of surrender.

sweet trade, the   buccaneering or piracy.

swivel (gun)   a gun mounted on a pivot so that it might be swung from side to side.

tender   a small boat, towed or carried by a ship.

top-gallant sheets   the sheets (ropes) attached to the sails of the top-gallant mast, i.e. the mast above the topmast.

Vice-Admiralty Courts   courts established in the British colonies for trial and decision of maritime questions and offences.

walk the plank   a method of disposing of prisoners at sea, said to have been much in vogue among the South Sea pirates of the seventeenth century, but not believed to have been used by the pirates of the West Indies.

warp   to move a vessel by hauling on a rope fixed to a stationary object ashore.

weigh (weigh anchor)   to raise a vessel's anchor preparatory to departure.

wherry   a light rowing boat, used in inland waters and harbours.

yards   the spars slung from the masts of a square-rigged vessel and used for suspending sails.

Main sources

Jamaica Archives
Records of the High Court of Vice-Admiralty Jamaica. Sessions of Oyer and Terminer.
Minutes of the Jamaica House of Assembly, and of the Council.
Plat Books.
Patents.
Calendar of State Papers, Colonial Series, America and West Indies (preserved in the Public Record Office). Edited by Cecil Headlam. HMSO, London 1933. Kraus Reprint Ltd, Vaduz 1964.
The Tryals of Captain John Rackham, and other Pirates. Printed by Robert Baldwin, Jamaica, 1721.

Berckman, Evelyn 1979 *Victims of Piracy, the Admiralty Court 1575–1678*, Hamish Hamilton, London.
Black, Clinton V. 1983 *The History of Jamaica*, Collins Educational, London.
Burney, James 1950 *History of the Buccaneers of America.* Reprinted from the edition of 1816, Allen & Unwin, London.
Burns, Sir Alan 1954 *History of the British West Indies*, Allen & Unwin, London.
Craton, Michael 1962 *A History of the Bahamas*, Collins, London.
Crump, Helen 1931 *Colonial Admiralty Jurisdiction in the Seventeenth Century*, Longmans, Green & Co., London.
Cundall, Frank 1936 *The Governors of Jamaica in the Seventeenth Century*, West India Committee, London.
Cundall, Frank 1937 *The Governors of Jamaica in the First Half of the Eighteenth Century*, West India Committee, London.
Esquemeling, Alexander Olivier 1923 *The Buccaneers of America.* Published in Amsterdam in 1678. Broadway Translations, London.
Gosse, Philip 1924 *The Pirates' Who's Who*, Dulau & Co. Ltd, London.
Gosse, Philip 1932 *The History of Piracy*, Longmans, Green & Co., London.
Hobsbawm, E.J. 1972 *Bandits*, Pelican Books, London.
Hurd, Archibald 1925 *The Reign of the Pirates*, Heath Cranton Ltd, London.
Johnson, Captain Charles [Daniel Defoe] 1972 *A General History of the Robberies and Murders of the Most Notorious Pyrates.* First published in London in 1724. Edited by Manuel Schonhorn, J.M. Dent and Sons, London.

[**Leslie, Charles**] 1740 *A New History of Jamaica*, J. Hodges, London.

[**Long, Edward**] 1774 *The History of Jamaica*, printed for T. Lowndes in Fleet Street, London.

McFee, William 1951 *The Law of the Sea*, Faber & Faber, London.

Mitchell, David 1976 *Pirates*, Thames & Hudson, London.

Parry, J.H. and **Sherlock, P.M.** 1956 *A Short History of the West Indies*, Macmillan, London.

Pope, Dudley 1977 *Harry Morgan's Way. The Biography of Sir Henry Morgan, 1635–1684*, Alison Press, London.

Pringle, Patrick 1953 *Jolly Roger. The Story of the Great Age of Piracy*, Museum Press, London.

Rediker, Marcus 1987 *Between the Devil and the Deep Blue Sea. Merchant Seamen, Pirates and the Anglo-American Maritime World, 1700–1750*, Cambridge University Press, Cambridge.

Roberts, W. Adolphe 1952 *Sir Henry Morgan. Buccaneer and Governor*, Pioneer Press, Kingston, Jamaica.

Winston, Alexander 1972 *Pirates and Privateers*, Arrow Books, London.

Woodbury, George 1954 *The Great Days of Piracy*, New York, 1951, London, 1954.

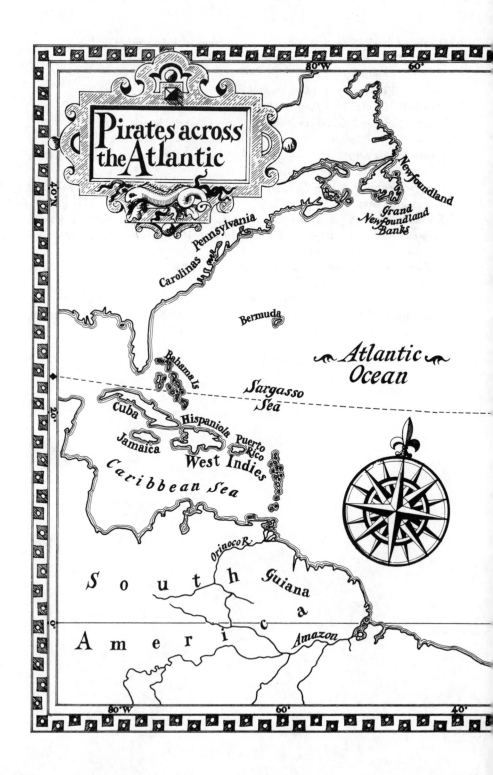

Pirates across the Atlantic

Newfoundland

Grand
Newfoundland
Banks

Pennsylvania

Carolinas

Bermuda

~ Atlantic ~
Ocean

Bahama Is.

Sargasso
Sea

Cuba

Hispaniola

Jamaica

Puerto
Rico

West Indies

Caribbean Sea

South

Orinoco R.

Guiana

a

A m e r i c

Amazon

80°W

60°

40°N

20°

0°

80°W

60°

40°

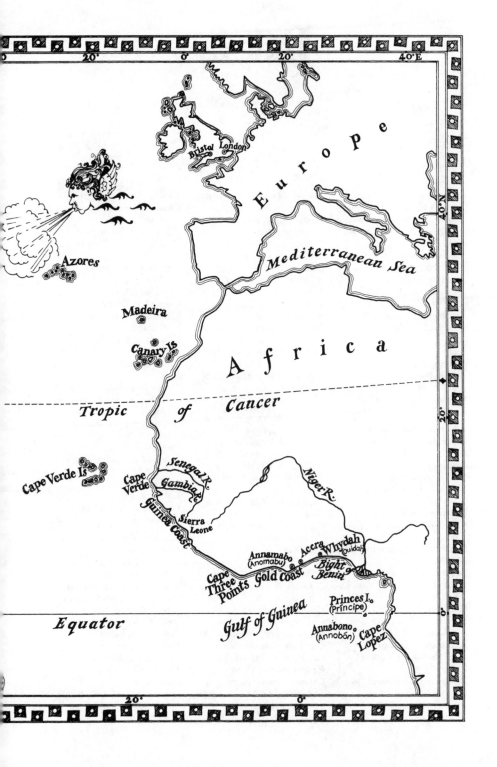

Index